Southern-Style
Style DIABETIC COOKING

Southern-Style DIABETIC COOKING

Marti Chitwood, RD, CDE

American Diabetes Association®

| **Book Acquisitions** | **Book Editor** |
| Susan Reynolds | Laurie Guffey |

| **Production Director** | **Production Coordinator** |
| Carolyn R. Segree | Peggy M. Rote |

Page design and typesetting services by Insight Graphics
Cover design by Wickham and Associates, Inc.
Cover photography by Aldo Tutino
Illustrations by Rebecca Grace Jones
Nutritional analyses by Nutritional Computing Concepts, Inc.

Printed in the United States of America

American Diabetes Association
1660 Duke Street
Alexandria, VA 22314

Library of Congress Cataloging-in-Publication Data

Chitwood, Martha, 1952–
  Southern-style diabetic cooking / Martha Chitwood.
    p.   cm.
  Includes index.
  ISBN 0-945448-69-4 (pbk.)
  1. Diabetes--Diet therapy--Recipes. 2. Cookery, American--Southern-style. I. Title.
RC662.C468 1996
641.5'6314--dc21   96-47060
                                                        CIP

Dedication

To all of the many, many special people who have touched my life because of diabetes.

Editorial Advisory Board

Wylie McNabb, EdD
The University of Chicago Center for Medical Education and
    Health Care
Chicago, Illinois

Virginia Peragallo-Dittko, RN, MA, CDE
Winthrop University Hospital
Mineola, New York

Jacqueline Siegel, RN
St. Joseph Hospital
Seattle, Washington

Tim Wysocki, PhD
Nemours Children's Center
Jacksonville, Florida

Contents

Preface

Chances are, since you picked this cookbook up out of the hundreds of cookbooks available at any given time, you probably have an interest in Southern-style cooking for people with diabetes. Maybe you have diabetes, or are cooking for someone who does. You'll be happy to hear that meals cooked Southern-style for those with diabetes do not have to be dull and tasteless! In fact, you might be surprised to find some of your classic favorites here: She-Crab Soup; Old-Fashioned Chicken and Dumplings; Red Beans, Ham, and Rice; Hush Puppies; and Date-Nut Sour Cream Pound Cake.

How can this be? It's simple. If you have diabetes, you're learning all you can about the healthiest ways to eat. Determine what works best for you (working with your health-care team), and figure out how to be flexible in your meal plan without compromising your goals. If you have some favorite foods you don't want to give up completely, learn how to incorporate them occasionally by balancing calories, carbohydrates, and fats in your other meals and snacks. This book will help you find that balance. Throughout this cookbook, I offer many hints about smart meal planning. You'll learn how to prepare nutritious and tasty versions of the foods you love, while still maintaining a commitment to the other healthy components of your lifestyle.

I am a Southerner, born and bred. I've been cooking Southern meals, and working with people with diabetes who want new and improved Southern recipes, for many years. I offer this book in the sincere hope that it brings more variety, satisfaction, and pleasure to your meals.

Acknowledgments

I would like to thank the following individuals for their generous support in the writing of this cookbook: Langdon Howard, Audrey Runey, JoAnne Milkereit, MS, RD, CDE, Connie Crawley, MS, RD, LD, and Nell Hair, RN, CDE, for their thoughtful reviews of the manuscript; Madelyn Wheeler of Nutritional Computing Concepts, Inc., who provided the expert nutritional analyses; Laurie Guffey and Susan Reynolds of the American Diabetes Association, for their ongoing input and feedback; Sherri Wilson, RD, who spent hours refining the manuscript; my many clients, who have graciously shared favorite recipes with me over the years; and most of all, my husband, Edmund, who tolerates my long hours, and cheerfully taste-tests all (well, most) of my recipes!

Introduction

Southern cooking has its roots in many cultures, including European and African. Pork and corn were two early Southern staples. From hogs came hams, pork shoulder, bacon (called white meat), lard (rendered pork fat), pig's head, pig's feet, and various organs (and don't forget the tail!). Corn was used in many foods, such as hoe cake, made of cornmeal, water, and lard (originally baked on a hoe in the fields, later fried in a skillet); ash cake, made of the same ingredients, but roasted over a fire; corn pone, a baked dish; roasted corn; succotash, corn mixed with beans; hominy, from corn grains soaked in lye, the water and hulls removed; and grits, which are dried, ground, and cooked hominy.

Africans introduced okra, black-eyed peas, collard greens, yams, sesame seeds, watermelon, and other fruits and vegetables. Other foods were brought from Central and South America, such as hot and sweet peppers, peanuts, tomatoes, lima beans, chocolate, white potatoes, and sweet potatoes. From China came oranges and peaches, and the West Indies contributed peppers and fruits.

During the Civil War, many Southerners relied on sweet potatoes, field peas, and greens for sustenance. There were shortages of many staples, such as salt, sugar, meat, and flour, and Southerners needed to be inventive and resourceful. Many recipes were developed to compensate for the missing ingredients, such as Mock Apple Pie, Acorn Coffee, and Eggless, Sugarless, Flourless Cake.

After the war, economic crises continued, and people made do with roots, beans, vegetation, and game. Some of the vegetables that helped Southerners survive were cabbage, okra, greens (turnip, mustard, and collard), pumpkins, squash, field peas, eggplant, pokeweed, corn, nuts (walnuts, pecans, and peanuts), and berries. To this day, these foods are the foundation of Southern cooking.

Almost every family kept a garden, so there was usually a ready supply of fresh vegetables. The warmer Southern climate allowed late fall harvests, which helped sustain people during the winter months. Low-cost meat products, including pork by-products, continued to be dietary staples. As supplies became more available, though, consumption of high-fat meats, as well as sugar and starches, became customary.

Today, you can still enjoy the flavor of traditional Southern cooking by preparing old favorites with newer, lighter ingredients. The recipes in this book are designed to be low in fat. Some of the modifications used in this book can be applied to other recipes. Experiment with some of your old favorites to help maintain a nutritious meal plan. Here are some tips and suggestions for how to prepare the healthiest, tastiest Southern meals.

Cut the Fat!
To reduce total calories and total fat in your meal plan, reduce the amount of calorie-rich ingredients. Generally, you can reduce butter, oil, or margarine by 25–75% in many dishes. Experiment with using 25–30% less fat first, then progress to 50% or even greater reductions. In some recipes, you can replace some of the fat with pureed vegetables or fruit (applesauce works well).

■ To decrease the saturated fat in your recipes, use monounsaturated oils (olive oil, canola oil, or peanut oil).

■ Use a nonstick cooking spray (preferably from a pump bottle) for sauteing or pan-frying. Olive-oil nonstick cooking spray is tasty.

■ Add small amounts of nuts, nut butter, seeds, or avocado instead of butter or margarine.

■ Try canola, soy, or fat-reduced mayonnaise, or make your own "light" mayonnaise by mixing equal parts of mayonnaise with one of the following:

✓ mustard

✓ skim or low-fat milk

✓ plain low-fat or nonfat yogurt

✓ fat-free sour cream

✓ blended 1% or fat-free cottage cheese

✓ blended tofu

Depending on the dish, you may be able to use pureed vegetables or fruits in place of some or all of the mayonnaise.

■ To reduce the fat content of meats:

✓ Cook chicken or turkey with the skin on (this will keep the meat moist and tender; the fat does not seep into the meat), but be sure to remove the skin before eating! Add seasonings underneath the skin to get the most flavor into the meat.

✓ Use a rack to drain off the fat when broiling, roasting, or baking.

✓ Keep meat portions modest, about the size of a deck of cards.

✓ Baste with juice, wine, or broth instead of butter or meat fat.

✓ Cook soups and stews enough in advance to refrigerate and skim off the fat before eating. If this is not practical, use a grease mop or a fat-removing pitcher before serving (both are usually available in kitchen specialty stores). Or try skimming the surface of the hot broth with an ice cube wrapped in a paper towel.

✓ Make gravies from the meat juices, not the fat. Or use a small, controllable amount of oil (1–3 teaspoons).

✓ Replace part of the meat in a recipe (up to half or more!) with beans, vegetables, or grains.

■ Enjoy more baked, grilled, or broiled seafood instead of fried.

■ Use soup stock, broth, or wine instead of fat to make delicious sauces. Replace fat with broth in casserole and stuffing recipes.

■ Use pureed vegetables, such as cauliflower, carrots, turnips, or potatoes, to thicken casseroles or soups instead of making rich cream sauces or a roux.

■ To reduce fat in fried recipes:

✓ Use a well-seasoned iron skillet (or other high-quality pan or fryer).

✓ Heat the pan before adding the oil—this prevents food from sticking to the pan.

✓ Use only fresh oil—never reheat oil and use it again.

✓ Use monounsaturated oils or nonstick cooking spray whenever possible.

✓ Heat the oil until it is hot, but not smoking (when fats reach the point of smoking, they begin to break down). If you place a food to be fried in underheated oil, much more fat is absorbed.

✓ Watch the pan closely, remove the fried item quickly, and drain it on several layers of paper towels. Pat out as much extra fat as possible.

✓ Serve light dishes for the rest of the meal: low-calorie vegetables, salad, and fruit for dessert.

Rethink Rich Dairy Products

Cream, milk, butter, and cheese are frequently used in Southern dishes. A healthy meal plan can generally accommodate the occasional use of real cream or butter, as long as the rest of the meal or day's meals are planned carefully. For every day, try these tips.

■ Use low-fat (1 or 2%) or skim milk whenever a recipe calls for milk.

■ For those people who need to use milk alternatives, try:

✓ Low-fat soy milk

✓ Low-fat rice milk

✓ Low-fat almond milk

✓ Tofu drinks (available at health-food stores)

Generally, these plant-based milk alternatives can be used in soups, desserts, and other dishes in equal amounts.

■ For cream and sour cream alternatives, try:

✓ Light or nonfat sour cream

✓ Replacing all or part of the cream with evaporated skim milk, skim milk, or a milk alternative

✓ Plain, unflavored nonfat or low-fat yogurt

✓ Blending 2 cups of low-fat cottage cheese, 2 Tbsp of lemon juice, and 3 Tbsp of skim milk until creamy

✓ Equal parts of low-fat cottage cheese and yogurt

✓ Using soft tofu (blend 12 oz with 1 Tbsp mayonnaise and 1 tsp of lemon juice for a creamier texture)

■ For a tasty alternative to butter or margarine, try this general purpose spread. Blend together 2 cloves of garlic, minced, ¼ cup olive oil, ¼ cup tamari, and ¼ cup toasted sesame seeds. Store the spread in the refrigerator, and use a small amount on bread or vegetables. This spread is strongly flavored and a little goes a long way!

Watch That Salt!

Too many salty foods can contribute to high blood pressure and heart disease. You may want to limit servings of foods that have more than 400 milligrams of sodium. To decrease the sodium levels in your meal plan, try seasoning foods with the following:

■ Use natural herb mixtures that you make yourself or that you purchase. Try growing your own herbs and enjoy the tasty results. Try these flavor combinations:

✓ Rosemary with peas, cauliflower, or squash

✓ Oregano with tomatoes, zucchini, or tomatoes

✓ Dill with tomatoes, green beans, peas, or potatoes

✓ Marjoram with carrots, spinach, or Brussels sprouts

✓ Chives with tomatoes, cucumbers, or potatoes

✓ Basil with tomatoes or eggplant

✓ Parsley, garlic, and onion with just about everything

■ Add an apple or a pear that has been cut up or pureed. The fruit provides a very subtle and pleasant sweetness to a pot of greens or other vegetables, so you won't miss the salt!

Make Desserts Special

It's not necessary to give up desserts entirely—just enjoy fresh fruit whenever possible, and include richer desserts in your meal plan occasionally. Plan in advance how to fit a dessert in. Try the above techniques for reducing fat in your dessert recipes. Have small portions of a dessert, and adjust for the added calories, carbohydrate, and fat by cutting down in the rest of your meal or day's meals. And get plenty of exercise! You'll feel better if you concentrate on healthier, more nutritious parts of your meal plan, but once in a while, savor a small portion of a special dessert!

Add Some Fabulous Fiber!

Overconsumption of refined flours, sugars, and fats means you're not getting enough of what your body needs to keep you healthy. To increase the fiber in a recipe:

- Add unprocessed bran to just about any recipe. You can generally replace about 25% of the flour in a recipe with bran. Or add a small amount of wheat germ.

- Use stone-ground flour and cornmeal in most bread recipes. Use whole-wheat flour instead of white. Some yeast bread recipes do not work well with all whole-grain flour—try using bread flour and add bran in these recipes. Or use half whole-grain flour and half white flour.

- Experiment with different flours, such as spelt or amaranth. Substitute part of the white flour with one of these flours:

  ✓ Quinoa

  ✓ Millet

  ✓ Spelt

  ✓ Brown rice

  ✓ Amaranth

  ✓ Buckwheat

■ Use old-fashioned and/or stone-ground varieties of cereal and grain items like oatmeal and grits. They take a little longer to cook but are definitely worth the effort! You can even replace half of the grits in a recipe with wheat bran— this adds great flavor.

■ Use pureed fruits and vegetables as substitutes for other ingredients. Try celery, yellow or green (zucchini) squash, cauliflower, or carrots in entrees, soups, and salads. Apples, peaches, and berries work well in sweet recipes.

■ To increase the overall nutritional value in recipes, always buy fresh produce, and cook it as little as possible to avoid destroying nutrients. Serve lots of raw vegetables and fruits.

Experiment with Soy

Eating soy products is associated with many health benefits, including lower blood pressure and lower blood cholesterol levels. Below are some soy foods you might want to include in your meal plan:

■ Tofu is soybean curd. This product is extremely versatile— it can be blended, marinated, stir-fried, grilled, baked, or used in desserts. It's a great protein source.

■ Tempeh is a cultured soy food, made from whole cooked soybeans mixed with other grains. It's a great meat substitute.

■ TVP (textured vegetable protein) is made from defatted soy flour. It can be used like ground meat.

■ Miso is fermented soy paste. It's great for flavoring soups, vegetables, stews, and stir-frys. Miso is rich in minerals, too. Use it in small amounts (1–2 tsp).

- Tamari is similar to soy sauce, but has aged longer. It's very high in sodium.

Enjoy Some Classic Southern Favorites

Some ingredients and flavorings are signature Southern. It's hard to imagine a Southern day without grits, greens, or red beans and rice. Include some of the following ingredients in your meals for that Southern touch. A chart summarizing the easiest way to cook light, Southern-style meals follows.

- Hot sauce flavors many recipes. In the past, hot sauce was made from small hot peppers, which were washed, trimmed, and put into glass jars. Hot vinegar was poured over the peppers, and they were allowed to "brew." The resulting sauce was then used over greens, rice, or meat dishes. There are virtually no calories in hot sauce, and the sodium content can be modest, so use it as liberally as your insides can stand!

- Butter beans are called by many other names: lima beans, butterpeas, bush peas, speckled beans, or sieva beans, to name a few. Traditionally, they are cooked with some kind of pork meat (bacon, fatback, or ham). Today, use a little bit of lean ham, a small amount of dry, crisp bacon, or skip the meat and make a very tasty dish using herbs and olive oil. Some folks like to toss a few pods of okra on top of a pot of butter beans just before serving.

- Crowder peas, cowpeas (black-eyed peas), and field peas (split peas) sustained many a Confederate soldier during the Civil War. These peas grow like weeds, tolerate drought and extreme heat, and could always be found. Prepare them like butter beans or green peas.

- Snap beans are that familiar favorite: green beans. They should be very fresh when prepared—you'll be able to snap them easily. For a quick, one-dish meal, plan for about ½ lb of snap beans, 2 or 3 small red-skinned potatoes, and one portion of lean pork or ham for each person. Place the beans, potatoes, and meat in a saucepot filled with boiling water and cook for 20–30 minutes. This dish is great served with another Southern classic, cornbread!

■ Benne seeds are more commonly known as sesame seeds. Considered a good luck plant, farmers often placed a few benne seeds at the end of each row of cotton to help yield a good crop. The seed is rich in nutrients, makes a nice wafer or cookie, and is great as a condiment. Use a sprinkle of toasted seeds on vegetables, cereals, or other dishes. (To toast, spread seeds on a flat pan and bake at 350 degrees for about 10 to 15 minutes.)

■ For a Southern New Year's Day, have some of the following, topped off with hot sauce, to guarantee yourself a fruitful New Year:

✓ Hoppin' John brings good luck.

✓ Greens ensure prosperity.

✓ Mustard brings purity.

✓ Benne seeds encourage steadfastness.

Instead of:	Try/Use:
Bacon slices	Soy bits (bacon-flavored) or 1 Tbsp finely chopped bacon
Bacon fat, shortening, lard, butter, or margarine	Olive oil, canola oil, peanut oil, nut butters
Cream	Evaporated skim milk, plain nonfat yogurt, blended tofu
Cheese	Reduced-fat versions
Salt, salty seasonings	Herbs, lemon, garlic, hot sauce
Regular bouillon and canned broth	Homemade stock, low-sodium broths, low-sodium bouillon powder
Regular mayonnaise	Nonfat yogurt, part mayo and yogurt, tofu
High-fat meats for seasoning (Ham hocks, fatback, bacon)	Lean ham, turkey bacon, lean pork chops, turkey wing (skin off), leftover chicken

Appetizers

Benne (Sesame) Seed Cocktail Wafers
Black Bean Dip
Chunky Avocado-Pineapple Dip
Crab Meat Dip
Creamy Cucumber Dip
Deviled Eggs
Hot Artichoke Spread
Low-Calorie Eggnog
Salmon Spread
Shrimp Paste
Spiced Pickled Shrimp
Spinach-Vegetable Dip

Benne (Sesame) Seed Cocktail Wafers

12 servings/serving size: 3 wafers
Preparation time: 20 minutes

Keep these delicious cocktail wafers in a covered tin or cracker jar, and pop into a warm oven to crisp before serving. (They are relatively high in fat, so use them sparingly.)

2 cups whole-wheat flour
½ tsp salt
Dash cayenne pepper
½ cup butter

¼ cup ice water
1 cup roasted benne
** (sesame) seed**

1. Preheat the oven to 300 degrees. Mix together the dry ingredients and cut in the butter. Add enough ice water to make a dough the consistency of pie crust. Add the benne seed.
2. Roll the dough out thinly and cut into small, round wafers. Place the wafers on a biscuit pan or cookie sheet and bake for 15–20 minutes until golden brown.

Starch Exchange	1	Cholesterol	22 mg
Fat Exchange	3	Sodium	182 mg
Calories	208	Carbohydrate	17 g
Calories from Fat	130	Dietary Fiber	4 g
Total Fat	14 g	Sugars	1 g
Saturated Fat	6 g	Protein	5 g

Black Bean Dip

8 servings/serving size: ⅓ cup
Preparation time: 15 minutes

Try serving this tasty dip with more unusual fresh veggies, such as jicama, rutabagas, or turnips. You can also experiment with different kinds of beans—try red, navy, or garbanzo beans in this recipe instead of black beans.

1 15-oz can black beans,
    drained and rinsed
1 small onion, coarsely
    chopped
1 small bell pepper, coarsely
    chopped

1 clove garlic, chopped
1 Tbsp red wine vinegar
1 Tbsp olive oil
½ tsp sugar
Fresh ground pepper to taste

Combine all ingredients in a food processor or blender. Process or blend until the beans are coarsely mashed.

Starch Exchange 1
Calories 73
   Calories from Fat 17
Total Fat ....2 g
   Saturated Fat ....0 g
Cholesterol ....0 mg
Sodium ....65 mg
Carbohydrate.....................11 g
   Dietary Fiber ....4 g
   Sugars..................................3 g
Protein..................................3 g

Chunky Avocado-Pineapple Dip

10 servings/serving size: ¼ cup
Preparation time: 5 minutes

Serve this light dip with fresh fruit wedges or celery strips.
Avocado is a great source of vitamins C and E.

**1 medium ripe avocado,
peeled and pitted**
**½ cup low-fat cottage
cheese**

2 Tbsp fresh lemon juice
**1 8-oz can unsweetened
crushed pineapple with its
juice**

1. In a food processor or blender, combine the avocado,
   cottage cheese, and lemon juice and process until smooth.
2. Place the puree in a medium mixing bowl. Add the
   pineapple and its juice. Mix well. Cover and chill for 2–3
   hours before serving.

Carbohydrate Exchange ....½
Monounsaturated Fat
 Exchange ....½
Calories 57
 Calories from Fat 31
Total Fat ....3 g
 Saturated Fat ....1 g

Cholesterol ....1 mg
Sodium ....48 mg
Carbohydrate........................6 g
 Dietary Fiber ....1 g
 Sugars.................................4 g
Protein..................................2 g

Crab Meat Dip

16 servings/serving size: 2 Tbsp
Preparation time: 15 minutes

Crab meat dip, both hot and cold, is served at many Southern restaurants as an appetizer. It will become a favorite at your house, too!

1 8-oz pkg Neufchatel cheese, softened	**1 Tbsp prepared horseradish**
Dash Worcestershire sauce	**2 Tbsp low-calorie French dressing**
½ cup lite mayonnaise	**½ tsp dry mustard**
8 oz cooked crab meat	**¼ tsp hot pepper sauce**
2 oz low-fat shredded cheddar cheese	**Dash paprika**

Combine all ingredients except the paprika and mix well. Sprinkle paprika over the top and serve.

Lean Meat Exchange	1	Cholesterol	26 mg
Saturated Fat Exchange	½	Sodium	206 mg
Calories	75	Carbohydrate	3 g
Calories from Fat	39	Dietary Fiber	0 g
Total Fat	4 g	Sugars	3 g
Saturated Fat	2 g	Protein	5 g

Creamy Cucumber Dip

16 servings/serving size: 2 Tbsp
Preparation time: 15 minutes

This dip is great with broccoli, celery, squash, or carrots.

2 medium cucumbers, peeled
   and grated
1 small onion, grated
1 8-oz pkg Neufchatel
   cheese, softened
2 Tbsp lite mayonnaise

½ tsp seasoned salt
¼ tsp garlic powder
½ tsp lemon juice
1 Tbsp chopped pimento
3 drops hot pepper sauce

1. Place the cucumber and onion on paper towels and squeeze until barely moist. Beat the Neufchatel cheese until smooth.
2. Stir in the grated vegetables and remaining ingredients. Chill before serving.

Saturated Fat Exchange........½	Sodium ....35 mg
Calories 23	Carbohydrate.......................1 g
Calories from Fat................16	Dietary Fiber ....0 g
Total Fat ....2 g	Sugars.................................1 g
Saturated Fat......................1 g	Protein................................1 g
Cholesterol........................5 mg	

Deviled Eggs

12 servings/serving size: 2 halves
Preparation time: 10 minutes

The best way to make sure you don't eat too many of these delicious deviled eggs is to only make enough to go around once!

12 hard-cooked eggs **3 Tbsp lite mayonnaise**
6 tsp vinegar **Fresh ground pepper to taste**
1½ tsp dry mustard **Dash paprika**

Cut the hard-cooked eggs in half lengthwise. Remove the yolks. Crush the yolks and mix with the vinegar, mustard, mayonnaise, and pepper. Refill the whites with the egg yolk mixture and garnish with paprika.

Medium-Fat Meat Exchange	1	Cholesterol	214 mg
Fat Exchange	½	Sodium	99 mg
Calories	91	Carbohydrate	1 g
Calories from Fat	59	Dietary Fiber	0 g
Total Fat	7 g	Sugars	1 g
Saturated Fat	2 g	Protein	6 g

Hot Artichoke Spread

6 servings/serving size: ¼ cup
Preparation time: 10 minutes

This is a light version of a very popular dip. Serve it with vegetables or whole-grain crackers.

1 14-oz can water-packed artichoke hearts, drained and chopped
1 5-oz can water chestnuts, drained and chopped fine

½ cup lite mayonnaise
½ cup grated Parmesan cheese
Garlic powder to taste

Preheat the oven to 350 degrees. Mix all ingredients together and put into an oven-proof ramekin. Bake for 20 minutes or until the mixture bubbles.

Vegetable Exchange	1	Cholesterol	13 mg
Fat Exchange	2	Sodium	389 mg
Calories	123	Carbohydrate	7 g
Calories from Fat	75	Dietary Fiber	2 g
Total Fat	8 g	Sugars	3 g
Saturated Fat	2 g	Protein	4 g

Low-Calorie Eggnog

4 servings/serving size: 1¼ cups
Preparation time: 10 minutes

Here's a delicious, low-fat version of a holiday favorite.

2 eggs, separated
4 cups skim milk
1 tsp vanilla
2 tsp sugar substitute

½ tsp brandy- or rum-
flavored extract
Dash nutmeg

1. Combine the egg yolks and milk in a saucepan. Cook over medium heat until the mixture coats a metal spoon. Cool.
2. Beat the egg whites until soft peaks form. Add to the milk mixture, then add the vanilla, sugar substitute, and extract. Mix lightly. Cover and chill.
3. To serve, pour the eggnog into cups and sprinkle with nutmeg.

Skim Milk Exchange	1	Cholesterol	111 mg
Fat Exchange	½	Sodium	158 mg
Calories	123	Carbohydrate	12 g
Calories from Fat	26	Dietary Fiber	0 g
Total Fat	3 g	Sugars	11 g
Saturated Fat	1 g	Protein	12 g

Salmon Spread

8 servings/serving size: ¼ cup
Preparation time: 10 minutes

This spread tastes great on thin crackers. Try adding paper-thin cucumber slices for a fancier hors d'oeuvre.

1 7½-oz can salmon
1 3½-oz pkg Neufchatel
cheese, softened
½ cup plain low-fat yogurt

3 drops liquid smoke
flavoring
3 Tbsp sliced green onion

1. Drain the salmon, reserving 2 tsp salmon liquid, and flake the salmon with a fork. In a separate bowl, combine the Neufchatel cheese, yogurt, liquid smoke flavoring, and salmon liquid. Blend thoroughly.
2. Stir in the green onion, then fold in the flaked salmon. Refrigerate at least 2 hours or overnight to blend the flavors before serving.

Medium-Fat Meat Exchange............1	Cholesterol......................24 mg
Calories 75	Sodium ....196 mg
Calories from Fat................39	Carbohydrate.........................2 g
Total Fat..............................4 g	Dietary Fiber ....0 g
Saturated Fat......................2 g	Sugars...............................2 g
	Protein...............................7 g

Shrimp Paste

8 servings/serving size: ¼ cup
Preparation time: 10 minutes

Any tearoom in the South is obliged to serve Shrimp Paste, an institution in these parts. Try spreading it over thin crackers, or make tasty cocktail sandwich morsels.

**1 lb boiled, deveined, and
    peeled shrimp
2 Tbsp lite mayonnaise
1 3½-oz pkg Neufchatel
    cheese, softened**

**5 drops Worcestershire sauce
Fresh ground pepper to taste**

Using a food processor or blender, mix all ingredients until the shrimp paste can be spread easily. The shrimp should be finely ground.

Medium-Fat Meat
    Exchange...........................1
Calories 79
    Calories from Fat................33
Total Fat ....4 g
    Saturated Fat.....................2 g

Cholesterol......................83 mg
Sodium ....177 mg
Carbohydrate......................2 g
    Dietary Fiber ....0 g
    Sugars...............................2 g
Protein.................................9 g

Spiced Pickled Shrimp

12 servings/serving size: 3 medium or 5 small shrimp
Preparation time: 15 minutes

Even though a large quantity of oil is in the marinade, only a small amount clings to the shrimp, making this a delicious, low-fat dish.

Jar of bay leaves
2 lb peeled, deveined, and boiled shrimp
6 small white onions or 2 medium yellow onions, thinly sliced
½ cup olive oil

¾ cup vinegar
2 tsp salt
½ tsp dry mustard
1 tsp Worcestershire sauce
Dash cayenne pepper
Dash pickling spices

1. In a crock or large bowl, layer the bay leaves (4–5 per layer), shrimp, and very thinly sliced onions. Alternate until all shrimp are used.
2. Combine the remaining ingredients and mix well. Pour over the shrimp. Cover and refrigerate for 24 hours, stirring occasionally.
3. Serve the shrimp with toothpicks in a bowl over ice as an hors d'oeuvre, or pile on a bed of lettuce and serve as a salad.

Very Lean Meat Exchange 1
Calories 35
  Calories from Fat 18
Total Fat ....2 g
  Saturated Fat......................0 g
Cholesterol......................37 mg
Sodium ....120 mg
Carbohydrate.........................0 g
  Dietary Fiber ....0 g
  Sugars.................................0 g
Protein..................................4 g

Spinach-Vegetable Dip

24 servings/serving size: 2 Tbsp
Preparation time: 15 minutes

1½ cup low-fat cottage cheese
¼ cup lite mayonnaise
½ cup chopped green onions
½ cup chopped fresh parsley
1 Tbsp dill
1 10-oz pkg frozen spinach,
   thawed and drained

¼ tsp hot pepper sauce
½ cup shredded carrot
1 clove garlic, minced
1 medium head red cabbage,
   raw

1. Combine all ingredients except the cabbage in a food processor or blender. Process or blend on high speed 1–2 minutes or until smooth. Chill the mixture overnight.
2. To serve, trim the core end of the cabbage to form a flat base. Cut a crosswise slice from the top of the cabbage, making it wide enough to remove about a fourth of the head.
3. Lift out enough inner leaves from the cabbage to form a shell about 1 inch thick. (Reserve the slice and inner leaves of cabbage for other uses.) Spoon the dip into the cavity of the cabbage and serve.

Free Food
Calories 19
   Calories from Fat 3
Total Fat ....0 g
   Saturated Fat ....0 g
Cholesterol ....1 mg

Sodium ....92 mg
Carbohydrate.......................2 g
   Dietary Fiber ....0 g
   Sugars................................1 g
Protein................................2 g

Soups & Stews

13-Bean Soup
Black-Eyed Pea Soup
Brunswick Stew
Carolina Oyster Stew
Gazpacho
Okra Soup
Potato-Kale Soup with Turkey Sausage
Pumpkin Soup
Seafood Chowder
She-Crab Soup
Split Pea Soup
Vegetable Broth
White Bean Soup

13-Bean Soup

12 servings/serving size: 1½ cups
Preparation time: 15 minutes

Bean mixes are very popular in the markets of Southern cities like New Orleans, Charleston, and Savannah. Any combination of beans will make a delicious soup.

2 cups 13-bean mix (omit seasoning packet sometimes included in mix)
½ lb smoked, center-cut pork chops, fat trimmed
3 quarts cold water
2 medium onions, chopped
3 celery stalks, chopped
3 cloves garlic, crushed

2 16-oz cans tomatoes, chopped
½ tsp pepper
⅛ tsp cayenne pepper
¼ cup dried parsley
2 bay leaves
⅛ tsp cloves
Dash marjoram or other dried herbs to taste
4 medium carrots, diced

1. Sort and wash the beans. Cover with water and soak overnight.
2. Drain the beans, rinse, and return to a large saucepot. Add all remaining ingredients except the carrots. Simmer for 1½ hours or until the beans are tender. Stir occasionally.
3. Add the carrots and simmer 20 minutes longer.

Starch Exchange...................1½
Vegetable Exchange................1
Very Lean Meat Exchange.....1
Calories 170
 Calories from Fat................13
Total Fat..................................1 g
 Saturated Fat.....................0 g

Cholesterol.........................7 mg
Sodium ....258 mg
Carbohydrate.....................29 g
 Dietary Fiber ....7 g
 Sugars................................6 g
Protein................................11 g

Black-Eyed Pea Soup

10 servings/serving size: 1½ cups
Preparation time: 20 minutes

1 lb dried black-eyed peas
4 slices bacon, chopped in
   1-inch pieces
1 medium onion, chopped
1 cup celery, chopped

1 Tbsp flour
2 qt water
1 medium tomato, chopped
1 small dried red pepper
2 cloves garlic, minced

1. Sort the black-eyed peas and wash well. Place in a large stockpot, cover with water, and bring to a boil. Boil for 2 minutes. Cover and let soak overnight.
2. Fry the bacon in a nonstick saucepan until crisp. Remove the bacon and drain well on paper towels. Discard the pan drippings.
3. Saute the onion and celery in the same saucepan until they are translucent. Remove them from the pan and set aside. Next, brown the flour in the pan, stirring constantly until it is golden brown (be careful not to let it burn).
4. Drain the black-eyed peas. Add all ingredients to the stockpot and cook over low heat about 2½ hours or until the peas are done, stirring occasionally.

Starch Exchange	2	Cholesterol	2 mg
Very Lean Meat Exchange	1	Sodium	56 mg
Calories	182	Carbohydrate	31 g
Calories from Fat	17	Dietary Fiber	5 g
Total Fat	2 g	Sugars	5 g
Saturated Fat	1 g	Protein	12 g

Brunswick Stew

8 servings/serving size: 1 cup
Preparation time: 5 minutes

You can use leftover cooked chicken in this quick stew.

6 cups low-fat, low-sodium chicken broth
1½ lb boneless, skinless, cooked chicken breast
2 large onions, chopped
2 cups cut okra
4 cups fresh chopped tomatoes or 32 oz canned tomatoes

1 cup lima beans
2 medium potatoes, diced
1 cup frozen corn
1 tsp salt
1 tsp fresh ground pepper
1 tsp sugar

Combine all ingredients in a large stockpot and simmer, uncovered, until the vegetables are tender, about 25 minutes.

Starch Exchange	1½	Cholesterol	67 mg
Very Lean Meat Exchange	3	Sodium	380 mg
Fat Exchange	½	Carbohydrate	25 g
Calories	255	Dietary Fiber	4 g
Calories from Fat	55	Sugars	9 g
Total Fat	6 g	Protein	26 g
Saturated Fat	2 g		

Carolina Oyster Stew

4 servings/serving size: 1½ cups
Preparation time: 25 minutes

1 Tbsp canola oil
1 large celery stalk with leafy
  tops, thinly sliced
1 small clove garlic, chopped
2 Tbsp flour
1 cup thinly sliced green
  onions

3 cups skim milk
2 8-oz jars oysters, drained,
  liquid reserved
1 tsp Worcestershire sauce
Dash hot pepper sauce

1. Heat the oil in a medium saucepan over medium heat. Add the celery and garlic and saute until they begin to soften (about 2–3 minutes).
2. Mix in the flour, then ½ cup of the green onions, and stir for 2 minutes. Gradually mix in the milk and reserved oyster liquid. Stir until the soup comes to a boil and thickens.
3. Add the oysters and Worcestershire sauce and simmer until the edges of the oysters begin to curl, about 3 minutes. Ladle the soup into bowls. Garnish with remaining green onions and serve. Let people add a dash of hot pepper sauce if they wish.

Starch Exchange.....................½
Low-Fat Milk Exchange..........1
Lean Meat Exchange..............1
Calories 213
  Calories from Fat................75
Total Fat ....8 g
  Saturated Fat......................2 g

Cholesterol.......................70 mg
Sodium ....247 mg
Carbohydrate.......................19 g
  Dietary Fiber ....1 g
  Sugars...............................13 g
Protein................................15 g

Gazpacho

8 servings/serving size: 1 cup
Preparation time: 20 minutes

Gazpacho is best served icy cold. You can garnish it with croutons, chopped tomato, diced cucumber, chopped avocado, lime wedges, or lite sour cream if you wish.

2 cloves garlic, peeled	3 Tbsp red wine vinegar
1 lb ripe tomatoes, chopped	1½ Tbsp olive oil
2 large cucumbers, chopped	2 cups ice water
1 cup finely diced bell pepper	Hot pepper sauce to taste
1 cup finely diced celery	Dash salt
½ cup finely diced onion	Fresh ground pepper to taste
2 cups tomato juice	Chopped parsley

1. Add the garlic, tomatoes, cucumber, bell pepper, celery, onion, and juice to a food processor or blender. Process until the mixture is smooth. Add the vinegar and olive oil and blend well.
2. Transfer the soup to a serving bowl. Stir in 1 cup of the ice water and chill for at least 4 hours. Before serving, stir in the additional water, season with hot pepper sauce, salt, and pepper, and garnish with parsley.

Vegetable Exchange................2	Cholesterol........................0 mg
Monounsaturated Fat	Sodium ....258 mg
Exchange ....½	Carbohydrate....................10 g
Calories 66	Dietary Fiber ....2 g
Calories from Fat................26	Sugars................................7 g
Total Fat ....3 g	Protein................................2 g
Saturated Fat......................0 g	

Okra Soup

10 servings/serving size: 1⅓ cups
Preparation time: 20 minutes

This hearty soup is a signature dish in the South. There are many variations using different kinds of meat. You can still make a good soup even if you omit the ham—try soy patties or another meat substitute. (The ham makes this soup relatively high in sodium.)

2 cups diced, cooked lean ham
3 qt water
2 medium onions, chopped
2 lb fresh okra, trimmed
1 large chopped bell pepper
2 28-oz cans whole tomatoes

1 cup fresh or frozen corn kernels
2 bay leaves
1 cup fresh or frozen lima beans
Fresh ground pepper to taste

Add all ingredients to a large stockpot and bring to a simmer. Continue to cook for 1–2 hours.

Starch Exchange	1½	Cholesterol	16 mg
Very Lean Meat Exchange	1	Sodium	659 mg
Calories	159	Carbohydrate	24 g
Calories from Fat	18	Dietary Fiber	6 g
Total Fat	2 g	Sugars	9 g
Saturated Fat	1 g	Protein	13 g

Potato-Kale Soup with Turkey Sausage

8 servings/serving size: 1½ cups
Preparation time: 30 minutes

This is definitely a one-pot meal. Add fresh, crusty bread, a crisp salad, and enjoy!

1 tsp olive oil
2 cups chopped onion
2 cups water
1 15-oz can low-fat, low-sodium chicken broth
2 cups peeled, cubed sweet potato
2 cups skim milk
¼ tsp salt
¼ tsp pepper
4 cups tightly packed, thinly sliced, fresh kale leaves
½ lb low-fat turkey sausage
¼ tsp fennel seeds, crushed (optional)
1 small clove garlic, minced

1. Heat the oil in a large stockpot over medium heat. Add the onion and saute 5 minutes. Add 2 cups of water, the chicken broth, and the sweet potato. Bring to a boil. Cover, reduce the heat, and cook 45 minutes or until the potatoes are tender. Remove from heat.
2. Using a slotted spoon, remove 1½ cups of the potatoes. In a food processor or blender, process the potatoes with ½ cup of the cooking liquid for 30 seconds or until smooth. Add the pureed potato mixture, milk, salt, and pepper back to the stockpot; stir well and set aside.
3. Combine the remaining 1 cup of water and the kale in a large nonstick skillet. Bring to a boil, then cover, reduce the heat, and simmer for 20 minutes or until the kale is tender. Add the kale and liquid to the potato mixture; stir and set aside.

4. Add the turkey sausage, fennel seeds, and garlic to the skillet; cook over medium heat until the turkey is browned, stirring to crumble. Drain the sausage and add it to the potato mixture, stirring well. Cook the soup over low heat for 15 minutes or until it is thoroughly heated.

Starch Exchange 1
Vegetable Exchange................1
Very Lean Meat Exchange 1
Calories 148
   Calories from Fat................37
Total Fat ....4 g
   Saturated Fat......................2 g

Cholesterol......................17 mg
Sodium ....448 mg
Carbohydrate.....................20 g
   Dietary Fiber ....3 g
   Sugars................................12 g
Protein..................................9 g

Pumpkin Soup

6 servings/serving size: 1⅓ cups
Preparation time: 15 minutes

This tasty soup looks beautiful served on a table decorated for fall. (It is relatively high in sodium.)

2 Tbsp canola oil
1 cup chopped onion
1 Tbsp flour
3 cups low-fat, low-sodium chicken broth
3 cups canned plain pumpkin (or cooked, fresh pumpkin)

½ tsp salt
Fresh ground pepper to taste
½ cup plain nonfat yogurt
Dash nutmeg

1. Heat the oil in a large stockpot over medium heat. Add the onion and saute for 5 minutes. Sprinkle in the flour; stir and cook 2 to 3 minutes.
2. Gradually add the broth and pumpkin, whisking thoroughly after each addition. Simmer gently about 15 minutes. Add the salt and pepper. Pour into warm bowls; top with a dollop of nonfat yogurt and sprinkle with nutmeg to serve.

Starch Exchange 1
Monounsaturated Fat
    Exchange...........................1
Calories 128
    Calories from Fat..............55
Total Fat................................6 g
    Saturated Fat.....................1 g
Cholesterol.......................1 mg
Sodium ....602 mg
Carbohydrate...................17 g
    Dietary Fiber.....................4 g
    Sugars...............................8 g
Protein................................4 g

Seafood Chowder

12 servings/serving size: $1\frac{1}{4}$ cups
Preparation time: 15 minutes

This tasty chowder is high in protein.

2 Tbsp canola oil
4 medium onions, chopped
1 large bell pepper, chopped
1 cup chopped celery
3 cloves garlic, minced
2 Tbsp whole-wheat flour
2 28-oz cans whole tomatoes
1 tsp sugar

1 tsp hot pepper sauce
$\frac{1}{2}$ tsp pepper
1 lb peeled and deveined
**   medium shrimp**
$\frac{1}{2}$ lb fresh crab meat
2 $6\frac{1}{2}$-oz cans minced clams
1 large fish fillet, cut into
**   bite-size pieces**

1. Heat the oil in a large stockpot over medium heat. Saute the onion, bell pepper, celery, and garlic until tender. Add the flour, stirring until smooth. Cook for 1 minute, stirring constantly.
2. Add the tomatoes, sugar, hot pepper sauce, and pepper and bring to a boil. Cover, reduce heat, and simmer for 15 minutes. Add the remaining ingredients, cover, and simmer an additional 15 minutes.

Starch Exchange 1	Cholesterol......................78 mg
Very Lean Meat Exchange 2	Sodium ....466 mg
Fat Exchange ....$\frac{1}{2}$	Carbohydrate......................14 g
Calories 167	Dietary Fiber ....2 g
Calories from Fat...............37	Sugars..................................8 g
Total Fat..............................4 g	Protein................................19 g
Saturated Fat......................0 g	

She-Crab Soup

4 servings/serving size: 1½ cups
Preparation time: 15 minutes

½ lb fresh crab meat
1½ Tbsp canola oil
¼ cup diced onion
2 Tbsp cornstarch
3 cups skim milk
1 cup low-fat, low-sodium
   chicken broth

½ tsp Beau Monde seasoning
⅛ tsp white pepper
Dash of mace
½ tsp hot pepper sauce
Minced fresh chives

1. Remove and discard the cartilage from the crab meat and set aside. Heat the oil in a large stockpot over medium heat. Add the onion and saute until tender.
2. Stir in the cornstarch and gradually add the milk, stirring constantly. Gradually add the broth. Cook over medium heat, stirring constantly, until the soup is thickened and bubbly.
3. Add the crab meat and the remaining ingredients except the chives and cook over low heat 10–15 minutes (do not boil), stirring frequently. Top with chives to serve.

Skim Milk Exchange...............1
Medium-Fat Meat
   Exchange..........................1
Monounsaturated Fat
   Exchange ....½
Calories 189
   Calories from Fat...............63

Total Fat ....7 g
   Saturated Fat......................1 g
Cholesterol......................52 mg
Sodium ....257 mg
Carbohydrate.....................15 g
   Dietary Fiber ....0 g
   Sugars................................9 g
Protein.................................17 g

Split Pea Soup

10 servings/serving size: 1⅓ cups
Preparation time: 15 minutes

You can substitute lentils for the split peas in this recipe for a tasty variation. Or, for a great presentation, make one batch of green pea and one batch of red lentil soup. Pour half of each into each serving bowl. With a knife, gently swirl the soups, creating an arty appearance!

1 16-oz pkg dried green split peas	½ cup chopped celery
2¾ qt water	2 bay leaves
4 small hot peppers	2 Tbsp olive oil
3 medium onions, chopped	¼ cup chopped celery leaves
2 medium carrots, diced	2 Tbsp chopped parsley

1. Sort and wash the split peas and place in a large stockpot. Add the water, cover, and bring to a boil. Cook 2 minutes. Remove from heat and let stand for 1 hour.
2. Add the remaining ingredients to the pot, bring to a boil, cover, reduce heat, and simmer for 1 hour. Serve immediately, or process the soup in a blender or food processor until smooth before serving.

Starch Exchange	2	Cholesterol	0 mg
Vegetable Exchange	1	Sodium	25 mg
Monounsaturated Fat		Carbohydrate	35 g
Exchange	½	Dietary Fiber	13 g
Calories	210	Sugars	8 g
Calories from Fat	30	Protein	12 g
Total Fat	3 g		
Saturated Fat	0 g		

Vegetable Broth

6 servings/serving size: 1 cup
Preparation time: 10 minutes

To make a Bouquet Garni, place your favorite dried herbs
(try parsley, bay leaves, rosemary, basil, and thyme) in a 6 x 6-
inch piece of cheesecloth. Tie the herb bundle with string
and drop into soup, broth, or stew for about 30 minutes!
Remove the Bouquet Garni and discard before serving.

2 qt water
1 large onion, chopped (add
   skins to broth)
4 stalks celery, sliced
1 large turnip or rutabaga,
   peeled and coarsely
   chopped

2 carrots, peeled and
   chopped
2 bay leaves
1 cup chopped parsley
1 Bouquet Garni (see above)

Combine all ingredients in a large stockpot. Bring to a boil,
then reduce heat to simmer. Cover and cook for 1 hour.
Strain and reserve the vegetables for other uses.

Free Food
Calories 13
   Calories from Fat 1
Total Fat ....0 g
   Saturated Fat ....0 g
Cholesterol ....0 mg

Sodium ....25 mg
Carbohydrate........................3 g
   Dietary Fiber ....1 g
   Sugars................................1 g
Protein................................0 g

White Bean Soup

8 servings/serving size: 1 cup
Preparation time: 30 minutes

2 cups dried navy or
  cannellini beans
1 large onion
4 whole cloves
4 cups water
4 cups low-fat, low-sodium
  chicken broth

2 bay leaves
2 Tbsp olive oil
2 large onions, chopped
1 cup chopped lean ham
2 Tbsp chopped fresh
  rosemary (or 1 Tbsp dried)
2 Tbsp chopped garlic

1. Place the beans in a large stockpot. Add enough cold water to cover and soak overnight. Drain well.
2. Return the beans to the pot. Add the whole onion, garlic, water, chicken broth, and bay leaves and bring to boil. Reduce heat and simmer for 45 minutes.
3. Heat the olive oil in a large skillet over medium heat. Add the chopped onion, ham, rosemary, and garlic and saute about 15 minutes. Add the mixture to the stockpot and simmer for another 30 minutes.
4. Discard the whole onion. Transfer 2 cups of the bean mixture to a food processor or blender and process until smooth. Return the bean puree to the soup and stir before serving.

Starch Exchange	2½	Cholesterol	10 mg
Lean Meat Exchange	1	Sodium	299 mg
Calories	263	Carbohydrate	37 g
Calories from Fat	54	Dietary Fiber	8 g
Total Fat	6 g	Sugars	7 g
Saturated Fat	1 g	Protein	19 g

Salads

Apple-Beet Salad
Citrus Gelatin Salad
Easy Coleslaw
Fruit Ambrosia
Grapefruit-Avocado Salad
Green Bean Salad With Sliced Tomatoes
Healthy Potato Salad
Herbed Shrimp Salad
Macaroni-Shrimp Salad
Marinated Cucumbers
New Waldorf Salad
Southern Chicken Salad
Spicy Crab Meat Salad
Spinach Salad
Sweet Potato and Apple Salad
Tomato Aspic

Apple-Beet Salad

6 servings/serving size: ½ cup
Preparation time: 10 minutes

If you use fresh beets, be sure to save the beet greens to use as a separate vegetable side dish. They're loaded with magnesium and other nutrients. You can steam or saute them in just 5 minutes.

2 cups shredded or chopped apple, unpeeled (Granny Smith work well)
1 15-oz can whole beets, drained and shredded or chopped, or 1 lb cooked beets, chopped

¾ cup sliced celery
1 Tbsp lemon juice
1 Tbsp honey
Lettuce leaves
3 Tbsp chopped walnuts, toasted

Combine all ingredients except the lettuce leaves and walnuts, tossing gently. Spoon out each serving onto lettuce leaves and sprinkle with walnuts to serve.

Fruit Exchange ....½
Vegetable Exchange................1
Polyunsaturated Fat
    Exchange ....½
Calories 76
    Calories from Fat................23
Total Fat..................................3 g
    Saturated Fat......................0 g

Cholesterol..........................0 mg
Sodium ....144 mg
Carbohydrate.....................14 g
    Dietary Fiber ....3 g
    Sugars.................................10 g
Protein.....................................1 g

Citrus Gelatin Salad

8 servings/serving size: 1 salad mold
Preparation time: 20 minutes

You can substitute finely shredded cabbage for the cucumber in this recipe. This is a tasty, low-calorie dish that can help offset a heavier item on your daily menu.

2 envelopes artificially sweetened lemon or lime gelatin
2⅔ cups water
½ cup vinegar
1 Tbsp lemon juice

1¼ cups thinly sliced cucumbers, peeled and cut into fourths
1 cup thinly sliced radishes
½ cup chopped celery
Nonstick cooking spray
Lettuce leaves

1. Sprinkle the gelatin over ⅔ cup of water in a saucepan; let stand 1 minute. Cook over medium heat, stirring constantly, until the gelatin dissolves. Stir in the remaining 2 cups of water, vinegar, and lemon juice.
2. Chill the gelatin until it is the consistency of unbeaten egg white, then fold in the vegetables. Coat eight ½ cup molds with nonstick cooking spray and pour the gelatin into each mold. Chill until solid. Serve on lettuce leaves.

Free Food
Calories 15
  Calories from Fat 1
Total Fat.................................0 g
  Saturated Fat......................0 g
Cholesterol ....0 g

Sodium ....60 mg
Carbohydrate........................3 g
  Dietary Fiber ....0 g
  Sugars..................................2 g
Protein...................................2 g

45

Easy Coleslaw

8 servings/serving size: ⅔ cup
Preparation time: 20 minutes

This light salad is a great accompaniment to many favorite Southern main dishes. You can add 1 chopped apple or ¾ cup chopped pineapple for a fruitier flavor.

**3½ cups shredded cabbage
(about ½ medium
cabbage)
½ cup shredded carrots
¼ cup chopped bell pepper
2 Tbsp minced onion**

**¼ cup chopped celery
¼ cup lite mayonnaise
1 Tbsp vinegar
½ tsp salt
½ tsp celery seed**

1. Combine all the vegetables in a large bowl. Mix well and set aside.
2. Mix together the remaining dressing ingredients, pour over the vegetables, and toss well. Refrigerate before serving.

Vegetable Exchange................1
Polyunsaturated Fat
    Exchange ....½
Calories 38
    Calories from Fat................22
Total Fat ....2 g
    Saturated Fat......................0 g

Cholesterol ....3 mg
Sodium ....212 mg
Carbohydrate.......................3 g
    Dietary Fiber ....1 g
    Sugars................................2 g
Protein..................................1 g

Fruit Ambrosia

10 servings/serving size: ½ cup
Preparation time: 10 minutes

You can also serve this fresh fruit salad as a light dessert.

**4 medium oranges, peeled
and sectioned
2 medium bananas, sliced
1 medium apple, diced**

**¼ cup orange juice
¼ cup shredded,
unsweetened coconut**

Combine the fruit and orange juice. Spoon into dessert
dishes and sprinkle with coconut to serve.

Fruit Exchange	1	Cholesterol	0 mg
Saturated Fat Exchange	½	Sodium	1 mg
Calories	82	Carbohydrate	17 g
Calories from Fat	19	Dietary Fiber	3 g
Total Fat	2 g	Sugars	12 g
Saturated Fat	2 g	Protein	1 g

Grapefruit-Avocado Salad

6 servings/serving size: ⅙ recipe
Preparation time: 15 minutes

This dish is high in mono- and polyunsaturated fat because of the avocado, walnuts, and mayonnaise. You can lower the fat content by reducing the walnuts to ¼ cup and substituting lite sour cream for the mayonnaise.

⅓ cup lite mayonnaise
2 Tbsp grapefruit juice
1 tsp honey
½ tsp grated grapefruit rind
1 medium avocado, peeled
   and sliced

Lemon juice
2 large grapefruit, peeled
   and sectioned
Bibb lettuce leaves
⅓ cup chopped walnuts
2 Tbsp currants

1. Whisk together the mayonnaise, grapefruit juice, honey, and grapefruit rind. Set aside in the refrigerator.
2. Dip the avocado slices in lemon juice. Alternate the grapefruit sections and avocado slices in a circular pattern on each of 6 lettuce-lined plates.
3. Divide the walnuts and currants in the center of each arrangement. Drizzle with dressing to serve.

Fruit Exchange 1	Cholesterol ....5 mg
Fat Exchange 2½	Sodium ....102 mg
Calories 168	Carbohydrate......................14 g
Calories from Fat 109	Dietary Fiber ....3 g
Total Fat ....12 g	Sugars.................................9 g
Saturated Fat.....................2 g	Protein.................................2 g

Green Bean Salad with Sliced Tomatoes

8 servings/serving size: ½ cup
Preparation time: 10 minutes

Green beans are heavenly right out of the garden. Their nutrient value is also highest when eaten fresh.

¼ cup vinegar, plain or flavored
¼ cup olive oil
Fresh ground pepper to taste
2 tsp grated onion

Fresh herbs of choice
1 lb fresh green beans
2 medium tomatoes, cut into wedges

1. Whisk together all ingredients except the green beans and tomatoes. Set aside.
2. Snip the ends off the beans and steam for 10 minutes. Immerse them immediately into ice water for 3–4 minutes. Drain.
3. Place the green beans in a salad bowl. Pour the dressing over the green beans, toss well, and refrigerate for 1 hour. Garnish with tomato wedges to serve.

Vegetable Exchange................1
Monounsaturated Fat
    Exchange........................1½
Calories 85
    Calories from Fat...............63
Total Fat ....7 g
    Saturated Fat.....................1 g

Cholesterol.........................0 mg
Sodium ....6 mg
Carbohydrate.......................6 g
    Dietary Fiber.....................2 g
    Sugars................................2 g
Protein................................1 g

Healthy Potato Salad

4 servings/serving size: ½ cup
Preparation time: 15 minutes

For a nice change of pace, try making potato salad with other root vegetables, such as turnips or rutabagas.

**2 medium potatoes, peeled
   and cut into ½-inch cubes
1 hard-cooked egg, sliced
¼ cup chopped celery
¼ cup chopped bell pepper**

**¼ cup chopped onion
2 Tbsp chopped pimento
1 Tbsp mustard
4 Tbsp lite mayonnaise**

1. Cook the potatoes in boiling water for 8–10 minutes until tender but still firm (be careful not to overcook!).
2. Drain and cool. Mix all ingredients together and chill before serving.

Starch Exchange 1
Fat Exchange 1
Calories 133
   Calories from Fat 55
Total Fat ....6 g
   Saturated Fat ....1 g

Cholesterol.......................59 mg
Sodium ....183 mg
Carbohydrate.......................15 g
   Dietary Fiber ....2 g
   Sugars................................3 g
Protein.................................3 g

Herbed Shrimp Salad

10 servings/serving size: ¾ cup
Preparation time: 30 minutes

The key to cooking shrimp is simple: always start with boiling water, and when the shrimp turn pink all over they are done! This only takes a matter of minutes. If you overcook shrimp, they become mushy and tasteless.

8 cups water
2 cloves garlic, chopped
3 bay leaves
1 Tbsp pepper
½ cup dry white wine
⅓ cup lemon juice

2½ lb peeled fresh shrimp
⅓ cup lite mayonnaise
1 tsp dill
¼ tsp white pepper
1 Tbsp spicy mustard
2 tsp lemon juice

1. In a large saucepan, combine the water, garlic, bay leaves, pepper, wine, and lemon juice. Bring to a boil, then simmer, uncovered, for 10 minutes. Skim off the spices. Return the water to a boil.
2. In 3–4 batches, put the shrimp in a strainer and lower into the spiced water. Poach gently for 2 minutes or until shrimp are pink and tender. Allow shrimp to cool.
3. Combine the remaining ingredients in a large bowl. Add the cooked shrimp and toss gently. Chill for 1–2 hours. Serve the salad on a bed of lettuce or in a hollowed-out tomato.

Very Lean Meat Exchange 3
Calories 109
   Calories from Fat 30
Total Fat ....3 g
   Saturated Fat ....1 g
Cholesterol ....163 mg

Sodium ....262 mg
Carbohydrate.......................1 g
   Dietary Fiber ....0 g
   Sugars.................................0 g
Protein................................17 g

Macaroni-Shrimp Salad

6 servings/serving size: 1 cup
Preparation time: 30 minutes

This dish is great to bring to summer potlucks or backyard barbecues. Add thin slices of avocado or wedges of tomato for a colorful touch.

$4\frac{1}{2}$ cups water
1 lb unpeeled, medium, fresh shrimp
$1\frac{1}{2}$ cups cooked elbow macaroni
1 cup frozen peas, thawed
2 hard-cooked eggs, chopped
1 medium bell pepper, chopped

$\frac{1}{2}$ cup chopped pimento
1 Tbsp chopped onion
$\frac{1}{4}$ cup lite sour cream
$\frac{1}{2}$ cup lite mayonnaise
$\frac{1}{2}$ tsp salt
$\frac{1}{8}$ tsp pepper
Lettuce leaves

1. Bring the water to a boil; add the shrimp and cook 3–5 minutes. Drain well and rinse with cold water. Chill. Peel and devein shrimp.
2. In a large bowl, combine the shrimp and all ingredients except the mayonnaise, salt, and pepper. Toss well. Whisk together the mayonnaise, salt, and pepper and pour over shrimp mixture, tossing gently. Chill. Spoon the salad onto lettuce leaves and sprinkle with paprika to serve.

Starch Exchange 1	Cholesterol.....................190 mg
Medium-Fat Meat	Sodium ....515 mg
Exchange............................2	Carbohydrate.......................18 g
Calories 234	Dietary Fiber ....4 g
Calories from Fat 86	Sugars..................................5 g
Total Fat ....10 g	Protein................................18 g
Saturated Fat ....2 g	

Marinated Cucumbers

6 servings/serving size: ⅔ cup
Preparation time: 10 minutes

This dish is always great to serve at picnics. Because it is low in calories, you can offset some of the richer foods on the table by including it!

4 cups thinly sliced cucumbers (see preparation step 1, below)
1 large onion, thinly sliced and separated into rings
1 cup water

1 cup vinegar, plain or flavored
1 tsp celery seed
½ tsp garlic powder (or 1 Tbsp chopped fresh garlic)
½ tsp salt

1. If the cucumbers are waxed, peel them before slicing. If they are not waxed and are chemical-free, leave the skin on. With a fork, score the sides of each cucumber, creating a ruffled edge. Slice thinly.
2. Layer the sliced cucumbers and onion in a large bowl. Combine the remaining ingredients and blend thoroughly. Pour the dressing over the cucumbers. Cover and chill at least 2 hours. Use a slotted spoon to serve.

Vegetable Exchange................1
Calories 28
  Calories from Fat..................1
Total Fat................................0 g
  Saturated Fat......................0 g
Cholesterol ....0 g

Sodium ....100 mg
Carbohydrate........................7 g
  Dietary Fiber......................1 g
  Sugars..................................5 g
Protein...................................1 g

New Waldorf Salad

6 servings/serving size: ⅓ cup
Preparation time: 15 minutes

Traditional Waldorf Salad uses a mayonnaise dressing base. You will be pleasantly surprised by the fresh taste of this version.

2 large apples, cored, unpeeled, and diced
2 tsp lemon juice
1 cup diced celery
¼ cup coarsely chopped walnuts

¼ cup black or golden raisins
¼ cup apple juice
Lettuce leaves

Toss the apples and the lemon juice in a large bowl. Add the remaining ingredients, mix well, and serve on lettuce leaves.

Fruit Exchange........................1
Polyunsaturated Fat
    Exchange............................1
Calories 99
    Calories from Fat................29
Total Fat...............................3 g
    Saturated Fat.....................0 g

Cholesterol.........................0 mg
Sodium ....21 mg
Carbohydrate......................19 g
    Dietary Fiber......................3 g
    Sugars..............................14 g
Protein..................................1 g

Southern Chicken Salad

6 servings/serving size: 1 cup
Preparation time: 15 minutes

This salad is a Southern classic. It makes a wonderful main dish for a brunch, luncheon, or supper meal.

3 cups chopped, cooked chicken (skin removed)
1 cup seedless grapes (about ½ lb)
½ cup chopped celery
⅓ cup slivered almonds, toasted
⅓ cup lite mayonnaise
⅓ cup plain low-fat yogurt
1 Tbsp lemon juice
¼ cup raisins or currants
⅛ tsp pepper
Lettuce leaves
Curry powder

1. In a large bowl, combine the chicken, grapes, celery, and almonds. Whisk together the remaining ingredients except the lettuce leaves and curry powder.
2. Add the dressing to the chicken mixture and toss well. Cover and chill. Spoon onto lettuce leaves and garnish with curry powder to serve.

Fruit Exchange	1	Cholesterol	69 mg
Lean Meat Exchange	3	Sodium	181 mg
Fat Exchange	1	Carbohydrate	16 g
Calories	273	Dietary Fiber	2 g
Calories from Fat	117	Sugars	12 g
Total Fat	13 g	Protein	23 g
Saturated Fat	3 g		

Spicy Crab Meat Salad

4 servings/serving size: 1 cup
Preparation time: 10 minutes

This light salad is great served as a main dish on a hot summer day. (However, it is extremely high in sodium.)

1 lb cooked crab meat
1 cup celery, diced
¼ cup lite mayonnaise
2 Tbsp reduced-calorie French dressing
1 Tbsp lemon juice

¾ cup chopped red bell pepper
¼ tsp Worcestershire sauce
Dash white pepper
Hot pepper sauce to taste
Lettuce leaves

1. Discard any bits of shell or cartilage in the crab meat.
2. Combine all ingredients in a large bowl; mix gently to avoid breaking the lumps of crab meat. Chill before serving on lettuce leaves.

Vegetable Exchange	1	Cholesterol	121 mg
Lean Meat Exchange	3	Sodium	855 mg
Calories	208	Carbohydrate	6 g
Calories from Fat	79	Dietary Fiber	1 g
Total Fat	9 g	Sugars	3 g
Saturated Fat	1 g	Protein	24 g

Spinach Salad

4 servings/serving size: ¼ recipe
Preparation time: 15 minutes

This salad tastes best with spinach fresh from the garden.

4 cups fresh spinach leaves, washed and torn
8 medium mushrooms, sliced
1 hard-cooked egg, chopped
2 slices purple onion, broken into rings
1 Tbsp imitation bacon bits or 1 strip cooked bacon, crumbled

2 Tbsp red wine vinegar
1½ Tbsp canola oil
1 tsp water
½ tsp dry mustard
½ Tbsp celery seed
⅛ tsp salt

1. Place the spinach on 4 individual salad plates. Top each salad with mushrooms, egg, onion, and bacon bits.
2. Whisk together the remaining ingredients and pour over each salad to serve.

Vegetable Exchange................1
Monounsaturated Fat
   Exchange.........................1½
Calories 102
   Calories from Fat................65
Total Fat ....7 g
   Saturated Fat.....................1 g

Cholesterol......................53 mg
Sodium ....162 mg
Carbohydrate........................6 g
   Dietary Fiber ....2 g
   Sugars.................................3 g
Protein...................................5 g

Sweet Potato and Apple Salad

6 servings/serving size: ¾ cup
Preparation time: 15 minutes

1 lb sweet potatoes, cut in half	½ tsp pepper
¼ cup white wine vinegar	2 cloves garlic, minced
2 Tbsp water	2 medium red apples, cored, unpeeled, and cut into 16 wedges
1 Tbsp canola oil	
2 tsp lemon juice	6 cups fresh spinach leaves, tightly packed
½ tsp sugar	
½ tsp salt	

1. Cook the sweet potatoes in boiling water for 25 minutes or until tender; let cool and peel. Cut into ¼-inch-thick slices and arrange in a large, shallow dish, overlapping slices.
2. Combine all remaining ingredients except the apples and spinach in a small jar; cover tightly and shake vigorously. Pour the dressing over the sweet potatoes; cover and let stand 1 hour.
3. Drain the sweet potatoes, reserving the dressing. Toss the apples with half of the reserved dressing. Arrange the sweet potato slices and apple wedges on each of 6 spinach-lined plates; drizzle with remaining vinaigrette.

Starch Exchange	1	Cholesterol	0 mg
Fruit Exchange	1	Sodium	245 mg
Calories	139	Carbohydrate	28 g
Calories from Fat	26	Dietary Fiber	5 g
Total Fat	3 g	Sugars	17 g
Saturated Fat	0 g	Protein	3 g

Tomato Aspic

6 servings/serving size: ½ cup
Preparation time: 20 minutes

This recipe is great with poached fish or chilled seafood or poultry. You can fill the center of the ring mold with boiled shrimp or marinated scallops and serve as a pretty appetizer.

2 envelopes unflavored
  gelatin
½ cup cold water
2 cups tomato juice
½ cup white vinegar
2 Tbsp sugar
½ tsp allspice

¼ tsp cloves
⅛ tsp pepper
Dash hot pepper sauce
1 small bell pepper, diced
2 Tbsp grated onion
Lettuce leaves

1. Sprinkle the gelatin over cold water and let stand for 1 minute. Combine the remaining ingredients except the bell pepper, onion, and lettuce leaves in a large saucepan and bring to a boil over medium heat.
2. Add the gelatin to the hot tomato juice mixture; stir until the gelatin dissolves. Chill until the mixture is the consistency of unbeaten egg white.
3. Fold in the bell pepper and onion; pour into a lightly oiled 4-cup mold. Cover and chill until firm. Unmold onto a lettuce-lined serving plate.

Vegetable Exchange................2	Sodium ....299 mg
Calories 47	Carbohydrate.....................10 g
Calories from Fat 1	Dietary Fiber ....1 g
Total Fat..................................0 g	Sugars...................................9 g
Saturated Fat......................0 g	Protein..................................3 g
Cholesterol........................0 mg	

Main Dishes

Baked Spareribs with Barbecue Sauce
Baked Stuffed Flounder
Black-Eyed Peas and Ham
Chicken Divan
Corned Beef Hash
Country Ham with Redeye Gravy
Crab Casserole
Hearty Meat Loaf
Low-Country Crab Cakes
Macaroni and Cheese Pie
Old-Fashioned Chicken and Dumplings
Oven-Fried Fish
Pasta with Blackened Shrimp
Poached Salmon with Cucumber Sauce
Pork Chops with Apple Stuffing
Red Beans, Ham, and Rice
Salmon Patties
Seafood Gumbo
Seafood Pie
Shrimp Fried Rice
Shrimp Perleau
Southern Fried Chicken
Spicy Sloppy Joes
Stuffed Baked Shrimp
Venison Chili

Baked Spareribs with Barbecue Sauce

6 servings/serving size: 3–4 oz
Preparation time: 15 minutes

This is a delicious version of a classic Southern favorite. You can also grill these ribs if you prefer.

2 lb lean pork spareribs
Fresh ground pepper to taste
Paprika to taste
Dry mustard to taste
1 clove garlic, minced
3 Tbsp vinegar
1 8-oz can tomato sauce

$\frac{1}{3}$ cup chopped onion
$1\frac{1}{2}$ tsp chili powder
$\frac{1}{2}$ tsp salt
$\frac{1}{4}$ tsp pepper
$\frac{1}{2}$ tsp oregano
$\frac{1}{2}$ cup water

1. Preheat oven to 325 degrees. Trim excess fat from ribs. Rub with a mixture of pepper, paprika, and dry mustard. Cut into 6 serving portions and place in a baking pan. Bake for 45–60 minutes. Remove pan from oven and pour off fat.
2. Combine the remaining ingredients and pour over the ribs. Cover and let stand 15 minutes. Return ribs to 350-degree oven and bake, covered, for $1\frac{1}{2}$ hours. Remove cover, baste, and bake for an additional $\frac{1}{2}$ hour. Spoon off excess fat before serving.

Vegetable Exchange.................1
Medium-Fat Meat
    Exchange..........................2
Calories 175
    Calories from Fat...............81
Total Fat ....9 g
    Saturated Fat....................3 g
Cholesterol......................57 mg
Sodium ....488 mg
Carbohydrate.....................5 g
    Dietary Fiber....................1 g
    Sugars..............................3 g
Protein..............................18 g

Baked Stuffed Flounder

4 servings/serving size: 4 oz
Preparation time: 30 minutes

2 Tbsp canola oil
¼ cup finely chopped celery
⅓ cup finely chopped onion
¼ cup finely chopped bell
    pepper
¼ lb cooked shrimp, diced
1 Tbsp chopped parsley
1 tsp finely chopped pimento
½ tsp paprika
½ tsp Worcestershire sauce

½ tsp Beau Monde seasoning
2 Tbsp dry sherry
⅛ tsp cayenne pepper
1 cup bread crumbs
4 small flounder, boned, or
    1 lb filets, very thin
2 Tbsp lemon juice
Fresh ground pepper to taste
¼ cup fine bread crumbs

1. Heat the oil in a skillet and saute the celery, onion, and
   bell pepper until tender. Add the remaining ingredients
   up to the 1 cup of bread crumbs and cook over low heat
   for 10 minutes. Add the bread crumbs and mix well.
2. Preheat the oven to 375 degrees. Stuff each fish with ¼ of
   the dressing or spread it over each filet. Roll and fasten
   with toothpicks. Place the fish in a nonstick baking pan
   and season with lemon juice and pepper. Sprinkle the
   bread crumbs over the fish. Bake for 25–30 minutes.

Starch Exchange 2
Lean Meat Exchange 3
Calories 334
    Calories from Fat 95
Total Fat .... 11 g
    Saturated Fat .... 1 g

Cholesterol .... 100 mg
Sodium .... 443 mg
Carbohydrate .... 27 g
    Dietary Fiber .... 2 g
    Sugars .... 3 g
Protein .... 30 g

Black-Eyed Peas and Ham

8 servings/serving size: ¾ cup
Preparation time: 10 minutes

To reduce the sodium content of this recipe, you could use lean pork. For vegetarians, seasoned, baked tofu, cut into squares, makes a tasty dish.

1 16-oz pkg dried black-eyed peas	1 cup chopped onion
3 cups water	1 cup chopped celery
¾ lb lean boneless ham, cut into ½-inch cubes	2 bay leaves
	1 tsp pepper

1. Sort and wash the peas and place in a large saucepan. Cover with water and bring to a boil; cook 2 minutes. Remove from heat. Let soak for 1 hour; drain.
2. Add the 3 cups water and remaining ingredients to the peas and bring to a boil. Cover, reduce heat, and simmer 1 hour or until the peas are tender. Remove the bay leaves before serving.

Starch Exchange	2½	Cholesterol	30 mg
Very Lean Meat Exchange	2	Sodium	1167 mg
Calories	285	Carbohydrate	37 g
Calories from Fat	39	Dietary Fiber	7 g
Total Fat	4 g	Sugars	6 g
Saturated Fat	1 g	Protein	26 g

Chicken Divan

4 servings/serving size: ¼ recipe
Preparation time: 20 minutes

1 Tbsp butter	½ cup bread crumbs
1 Tbsp cornstarch	¼ cup lite mayonnaise
1 cup skim milk	½ tsp curry
⅛ tsp white pepper	2 Tbsp lemon juice
8 oz boneless, skinless,	4 Tbsp Parmesan cheese
cooked chicken breast	Dash paprika
1 bunch broccoli, cut into	
1-inch pieces and steamed	

1. Preheat the oven to 350 degrees. Melt the butter in a saucepot. Add the cornstarch, stirring constantly. Add the milk in small batches, mixing well after each addition. Cook over medium heat until thickened, about 4–5 minutes. Add the pepper.
2. Whisk together the mayonnaise, curry, and lemon juice. Place a layer of chicken, broccoli, and bread crumbs in a nonstick casserole dish.
3. Spread the mayonnaise mixture over the chicken layer. Pour the cream sauce on top, then add cheese. Sprinkle paprika over the casserole and bake until hot and bubbly, about 20 minutes.

Starch Exchange 1	Cholesterol......................67 mg
Vegetable Exchange.................1	Sodium ....448 mg
Lean Meat Exchange..............3	Carbohydrate.....................20 g
Fat Exchange ....½	Dietary Fiber ....3 g
Calories 302	Sugars................................5 g
Calories from Fat..............111	Protein...............................26 g
Total Fat...............................12 g	
Saturated Fat.......................4 g	

Corned Beef Hash

2 servings/serving size: ½ recipe
Preparation time: 15 minutes

This hash is great for a quick weekend breakfast. (It is, however, high in sodium and fat.)

2 tsp canola oil
1 cup cooked, cubed corned beef, fat trimmed
1 cup peeled, cubed potato
2 cups chopped cabbage

½ cup chopped onion
2 Tbsp chopped parsley
½ cup bell pepper
¼ tsp pepper

Heat the oil in a large skillet over medium-high heat. Add all ingredients and cook, stirring occasionally, for 10 minutes or until mixture is browned and potatoes are tender. Reduce the heat, cover, and simmer for 4–5 more minutes.

Starch Exchange 1
Vegetable Exchange................1
Medium-Fat Meat
   Exchange............................2
Fat Exchange 1½
Calories 323
   Calories from Fat..............167
Total Fat ....19 g
   Saturated Fat......................5 g

Cholesterol......................69 mg
Sodium ....823 mg
Carbohydrate....................24 g
   Dietary Fiber ....4 g
   Sugars..................................8 g
Protein...............................16 g

Country Ham with Redeye Gravy

2 servings/serving size: 3 oz
Preparation time: 10 minutes

This dish is a Southern favorite, but extremely high in sodium, so save it for special occasions! To reduce the sodium content, soak the ham in water overnight and pat dry before cooking.

**2 3-oz slices uncooked lean
   ham, fat trimmed
1 Tbsp canola oil
1 cup strong black coffee**

**1 Tbsp brown sugar
2 Tbsp flour
$\frac{1}{2}$ tsp paprika**

1. Heat the oil in a skillet and saute the ham on each side for 3–4 minutes. Remove the ham from the skillet and keep warm.
2. Combine the coffee, brown sugar, and flour. Add to the pan drippings, stirring constantly, until thickened. Add the paprika. Serve the gravy with the ham.

Starch Exchange 1	Cholesterol......................46 mg
Medium-Fat Meat	Sodium ....1182 mg
Exchange............................2	Carbohydrate......................14 g
Fat Exchange 1½	Dietary Fiber ....0 g
Calories 294	Sugars................................7 g
Calories from Fat..............165	Protein................................18 g
Total Fat ....18 g	
Saturated Fat......................4 g	

Crab Casserole

4 servings/serving size: ¼ recipe
Preparation time: 10 minutes

You could easily substitute scallops, shrimp, or oysters in this bubbly casserole. (This dish is extremely high in sodium.)

1 can reduced-fat cream of mushroom soup, undiluted
1 8-oz can crab meat
½ cup prepared stuffing mix
½ cup chopped bell pepper
½ cup chopped celery
½ cup lite mayonnaise
Hot pepper sauce to taste
Cajun spice to taste

Preheat the oven to 350 degrees. Combine all ingredients and bake in a casserole dish for 1 hour.

Starch Exchange 1
Lean Meat Exchange 1
Polyunsaturated Fat
    Exchange 2
Calories 221
    Calories from Fat 112
Total Fat .... 12 g
    Saturated Fat .... 2 g

Cholesterol .... 63 mg
Sodium .... 1017 mg
Carbohydrate .... 13 g
    Dietary Fiber .... 1 g
    Sugars .... 3 g
Protein .... 11 g

Hearty Meat Loaf

6 servings/serving size: 1 slice
Preparation time: 10 minutes

Here's a favorite Southern meal: homemade mashed potatoes, turnip greens, and meat loaf. Try to have about twice as much greens as potatoes and meat loaf!

½ cup low-fat, low-sodium beef broth
2 slices whole-wheat bread, finely crumbled
1 lb extra lean ground beef
2 medium eggs, beaten slightly

½ cup finely chopped onion
½ cup finely chopped celery
½ cup grated carrots
2 tsp Worcestershire sauce
1 tsp dry mustard
1 Tbsp catsup
Fresh ground pepper to taste

1. Preheat the oven to 350 degrees. Line a 8 x 8-inch baking pan with foil. Heat the broth in a large saucepan. Add all ingredients except the catsup and pepper and blend well with a fork.
2. Add the mixture to the baking pan and pat it quickly into the shape of the pan. Sprinkle with pepper and spread the catsup on top. Cover with foil and bake for 45 minutes. Remove the foil and bake, uncovered, for another 30 minutes.

Starch Exchange....................½
Medium-Fat Meat
    Exchange...........................2
Fat Exchange ....½
Calories 212
    Calories from Fat..............102
Total Fat..............................11 g
    Saturated Fat......................4 g
Cholesterol....................118 mg
Sodium ....225 mg
Carbohydrate........................9 g
    Dietary Fiber......................1 g
Sugars...................................2 g
Protein................................18 g

Low-Country Crab Cakes

4 servings/serving size: 1 crab cake
Preparation time: 10 minutes

Serve this recipe with Seafood Herb Dressing (see recipe, p. 127). It tastes best when made with fresh crab meat.

1 medium red pepper, chopped fine
1 lb lump crab meat
3 slices bread, toasted and crumbled
1 egg
1 Tbsp minced fresh tarragon
1 Tbsp minced fresh parsley
2 tsp chives
White pepper to taste
Paprika to taste
1/3 cup lite mayonnaise
Nonstick cooking spray

1. Mix all ingredients except the mayonnaise and cooking spray together in a small bowl. Add the mayonnaise and toss lightly to mix. Refrigerate for 1 hour so the flavors will blend.
2. Form the mixture into 4 cakes. Spray a skillet with nonstick cooking spray and saute the crab cakes on each side until golden brown.

Starch Exchange 1
Lean Meat Exchange..............3
Calories 244
  Calories from Fat................88
Total Fat..............................10 g
  Saturated Fat....................2 g
Cholesterol....................158 mg
Sodium ....534 mg
Carbohydrate.....................13 g
  Dietary Fiber ....1 g
Sugars................................3 g
Protein................................23 g

Macaroni and Cheese Pie

8 servings/serving size: ½ cup
Preparation time: 10 minutes

This low-fat version of a stick-to-your-ribs favorite is just as satisfying.

2 cups skim milk
2 eggs
1 Tbsp canola oil

1 tsp pepper
6 oz low-fat cheddar cheese
2½ cups cooked macaroni

1. Preheat the oven to 350 degrees. Combine the milk, eggs, oil, and pepper in a bowl. Add the cheese and macaroni.
2. Spray a 9-inch pie pan with nonstick cooking spray and pour the mixture in the pan. Bake for 40–50 minutes until bubbly.

Starch Exchange 1
Very Lean Meat Exchange 2
Fat Exchange ....½
Calories 178
   Calories from Fat 58
Total Fat ....6 g
   Saturated Fat ....2 g

Cholesterol ....65 mg
Sodium ....168 mg
Carbohydrate....................16 g
   Dietary Fiber ....1 g
   Sugars...............................3 g
Protein................................12 g

71

Old-Fashioned Chicken and Dumplings

8 servings/serving size: 3 oz chicken with 1 dumpling
Preparation time: 30 minutes

Serve this nostalgic dish with fresh carrots, green beans, or juicy, sliced tomatoes.

1 3-lb stewing chicken, skin removed (to yield about 1½ lb of meat)
2 small onions, sliced
3 carrots, sliced
3 celery ribs with leaves
White pepper to taste
6 cups water

1 cup whole-wheat flour
½ cup unprocessed, uncooked wheat bran
1 tsp baking powder
⅛ tsp paprika
¼ tsp salt
3 Tbsp butter

1. Simmer the chicken, onion, carrot, celery, and pepper in the water until the chicken is done, about 1½–2 hours. Remove the chicken from the broth.
2. When it is cool enough to handle, bone the chicken and cut the meat into bite-size pieces. Set aside the meat and ⅓ cup broth.
3. Combine the flour, ¼ cup of the bran, baking powder, paprika, and salt. Cut in the butter. Add the ⅓ cup cooled broth to make a soft dough. Knead 3–4 times.
4. Turn the dough out onto a surface covered with the remaining bran. Pat out to a ½ inch thickness. Cut into squares or biscuits.
5. Bring the remaining broth to a boil. Drop the dough, one piece at a time, into the boiling broth, gently stirring after each addition. Cook for 8–10 minutes.

6. Serve the chicken in a bowl, topped with dumplings.

Starch Exchange 1

Lean Meat Exchange...............2

Fat Exchange ....½

Calories 216

   Calories from Fat................87

Total Fat...............................10 g

   Saturated Fat.......................4 g

Cholesterol.......................69 mg

Sodium ....220 mg

Carbohydrate.....................12 g

   Dietary Fiber ....3 g

   Sugars...................................0 g

Protein.................................21 g

Oven-Fried Fish

4 servings/serving size: 4 oz
Preparation time: 10 minutes

Try a light tartar sauce to go with this fish: combine ¼ cup lite mayonnaise, ¼ cup nonfat plain yogurt, 2 Tbsp sweet relish, 2 Tbsp grated onion, and 1 Tbsp lemon juice. Combine all ingredients and chill before serving. (Nutrient analysis not included.)

1 lb halibut, cod, or flounder
1 can beer
2 Tbsp canola oil
½ cup bread crumbs

3 Tbsp minced fresh parsley
1 tsp paprika
½ tsp salt

1. Marinate the fish in the beer for 60 minutes. Drain and pat the fish dry. Preheat the oven to 350 degrees.
2. Brush the fish with oil. Combine the remaining ingredients, and dredge the fish in the mixture until completely covered.
3. Place the fish in a nonstick baking pan and bake for 15–20 minutes, or until the fish flakes easily.

Starch Exchange 1
Medium-Fat Meat
   Exchange............................2
Monounsaturated Fat
   Exchange............................1
Calories 279
   Calories from Fat..............145
Total Fat..............................16 g
   Saturated Fat......................3 g

Cholesterol.......................65 mg
Sodium ....491 mg
Carbohydrate......................12 g
   Dietary Fiber ....1 g
   Sugars.................................2 g
Protein...............................21 g

Pasta with Blackened Shrimp

4 servings/serving size: ½ cup pasta with 4 oz shrimp
Preparation time: 15 minutes

5 Tbsp olive oil
2 green onions, chopped
1 clove garlic, chopped
4 medium tomatoes, chopped fine
1 lb peeled, uncooked, small shrimp

Salt-free Cajun blackening spice
2 cups cooked pasta of your choice (small shells are nice)
¼ cup chopped fresh cilantro or parsley

1. Heat 2 Tbsp of the oil in a skillet over medium heat. Add the green onions and garlic and saute until golden. Add the tomato and cook just until the tomato softens (it should remain chunky).
2. Coat the shrimp with Cajun spice. Heat 3 Tbsp of oil in a black iron skillet to very hot. Add the shrimp and quickly cook shrimp just until tender (2–3 minutes). To serve, pour the tomato sauce over the pasta, add shrimp on top of the sauce, and sprinkle cilantro or parsley over the shrimp.

Starch Exchange 3
Vegetable Exchange................1
Medium-Fat Meat Exchange............................2
Monounsaturated Fat Exchange........................1½
Calories 479
   Calories from Fat..............173

Total Fat...............................19 g
   Saturated Fat.......................3 g
Cholesterol....................166 mg
Sodium ....211 mg
Carbohydrate......................50 g
   Dietary Fiber ....3 g
   Sugars................................7 g
Protein................................26 g

Poached Salmon with Cucumber Sauce

6 servings/serving size: 3–4 oz
Preparation time: 15 minutes

You can also serve this poached salmon as a hot dish.

1½ lb boneless, skinless,
   fresh salmon
1 quart water
2 bay leaves
1 lemon, sliced
3 celery ribs, chopped
1 large onion, sliced
1 tsp canola oil

¼ tsp pepper
1 cup lite mayonnaise
3 Tbsp lemon juice
¼ tsp curry powder
Dash hot pepper sauce
½ cup finely chopped
   cucumber

1. Pour the water into a roasting pan large enough to hold the salmon. Add the bay leaves, lemon, celery, onion, oil, and pepper and bring to a boil. Add the salmon, reduce heat to simmer, and poach the salmon about 20 minutes or until the fish flakes easily when pierced with a fork.
2. Cool the salmon in the stock. Remove the salmon and drain it on paper towels, then refrigerate until cold. (You can reuse the stock in a seafood soup or chowder.) To make the sauce, combine all remaining ingredients. Chill before serving with the salmon.

Medium-Fat Meat
   Exchange............................4
Calories 312
   Calories from Fat..............175
Total Fat..............................19 g
   Saturated Fat......................3 g

Cholesterol......................70 mg
Sodium ....346 mg
Carbohydrate........................3 g
   Dietary Fiber ....0 g
   Sugars..................................2 g
Protein..............................27 g

Pork Chops with Apple Stuffing

6 servings/serving size: 3 oz
Preparation time: 10 minutes

You'll enjoy the complementary flavors of apple and pork!

1 Tbsp canola oil	2 small apples, cored and
18 oz boneless pork chops	chopped
1 cup prepared stuffing mix	$\frac{1}{4}$ cup onion, chopped
$\frac{1}{2}$ cup raisins, chopped	1 low-sodium bouillon cube
1 cup celery, chopped	$1\frac{1}{2}$ cups hot water

1. Preheat the oven to 350 degrees. Heat the oil in a medium skillet and brown the pork chops for 3–4 minutes on each side. Remove them and place in a nonstick baking dish.
2. In a medium bowl, combine the remaining ingredients except the bouillon and water. Dissolve the bouillon cube in the hot water, then add to the dressing mixture and mix well. Spread the dressing over the pork chops. Cover the baking dish with foil and bake for 50 minutes.

Starch Exchange	2	Cholesterol	66 mg
Lean Meat Exchange	3	Sodium	366 mg
Calories	312	Carbohydrate	27 g
Calories from Fat	98	Dietary Fiber	3 g
Total Fat	11 g	Sugars	14 g
Saturated Fat	3 g	Protein	26 g

Red Beans, Ham, and Rice

12 servings/serving size: ¾ cup beans with ⅓ cup rice
Preparation time: 20 minutes

Add "heat" (hot pepper sauce) to taste. Many Southerners compete to see who can handle the most heat. If you're brave, try different hot sauces, such as jalapeno or fiery green sauce.

1 lb dried red beans	½ tsp cayenne pepper
1 Tbsp olive oil	1 tsp sage
2½ cups chopped celery	½ tsp pepper
2 cups diced onion	1 tsp hot pepper sauce
1 cup sliced green onion	(optional)
1 cup chopped bell pepper	2 bay leaves
4 cloves garlic, minced	2 qt water
6 oz diced, cooked, lean ham	4 cups hot cooked rice

1. Sort and wash the beans and place them in a large pot. Cover with water 2 inches above the beans; let soak 8 hours. Drain. Heat the oil in a large stockpot over medium-high heat. Add the celery, onion, green onion, bell pepper, and garlic and saute until tender.
2. Add the remaining ingredients except the rice and cook, uncovered, over medium heat for 1–1½ hours, stirring occasionally. Remove the bay leaves and serve over rice.

Starch Exchange	2½	Cholesterol	8 mg
Very Lean Meat Exchange	1	Sodium	214 mg
Calories	240	Carbohydrate	41 g
Calories from Fat	22	Dietary Fiber	7 g
Total Fat	2 g	Sugars	3 g
Saturated Fat	1 g	Protein	14 g

Salmon Patties

4 servings/serving size: 1 patty
Preparation time: 10 minutes

This recipe is relatively high in sodium.

1 16-oz can salmon
1 Tbsp lemon juice
Cold water
2 medium eggs, beaten
Dash pepper
1 slice bread, finely
    crumbled
¼ cup finely minced celery
    and leaves

2 Tbsp finely minced green
    onion
1 Tbsp finely minced bell
    pepper
⅓ cup chopped onion
2 Tbsp flour
1 tsp baking powder
2 Tbsp canola oil

1. Preheat the oven to 350 degrees. Drain the salmon, reserving the liquid. Discard the skin, but save the bones. Flake the salmon lightly, but well, with a fork. Crush the bones and mix with the salmon.
2. Add the lemon to the reserved salmon liquid and enough cold water to make ½ cup liquid; add to the salmon. Add all remaining ingredients and mix thoroughly. Form into 4 patties. Bake for 25–30 minutes.

Starch Exchange.....................½
Lean Meat Exchange..............4
Fat Exchange 1
Calories 302
    Calories from Fat..............154
Total Fat ....17 g
    Saturated Fat......................4 g

Cholesterol....................169 mg
Sodium ....790 mg
Carbohydrate.........................9 g
    Dietary Fiber ....1 g
    Sugars..................................2 g
Protein.................................27 g

Seafood Gumbo

10 servings/serving size: 1¼ cups
Preparation time: 30 minutes

4 Tbsp olive oil
1 lb fresh okra, sliced (or 2 10-oz pkgs frozen, sliced okra)
4 Tbsp whole-wheat flour
1 cup chopped onion
1 cup chopped celery
1 cup chopped bell pepper
2 cloves garlic, minced
2 16-oz cans tomatoes, undrained
4 cups water

¼ tsp cayenne pepper
½ tsp salt
½ tsp pepper
Bay leaf
1 Tbsp gumbo file spice (sassafras leaves)
2 lb raw, shelled seafood (try using a combination, like 1 lb peeled shrimp, ½ lb crab meat, and ½ lb red snapper)

1. Heat 2 Tbsp of the oil in a large skillet and saute the okra until slightly browned. Set the okra aside. Combine the remaining 2 Tbsp oil and the flour in the skillet and cook over medium heat, stirring constantly, until the roux is medium brown in color (this takes about 20 minutes).
2. Stir in the onion, celery, bell pepper, garlic, and okra and cook until the vegetables are tender. Transfer the mixture to a large stockpot and add the remaining ingredients. Bring to a boil, then reduce heat and simmer, uncovered, for about 1 hour, stirring occasionally.

Starch Exchange	1	Cholesterol	97 mg
Lean Meat Exchange	2	Sodium	300 mg
Fat Exchange	½	Carbohydrate	12 g
Calories	187	Dietary Fiber	3 g
Calories from Fat	70	Sugars	5 g
Total Fat	8 g	Protein	18 g
Saturated Fat	1 g		

Seafood Pie

10 servings/serving size: 1 slice
Preparation time: 30 minutes

2 cups low-fat, low-sodium
  chicken broth
½ lb scallops
½ lb halibut or flounder,
  diced
½ cup crab meat
½ cup lobster, cooked and
  cut into bite-size pieces
2 Tbsp canola oil

½ cup chopped onion
2 cups celery, finely diced
3 Tbsp flour
¼ cup dry sherry
Fresh ground pepper to taste
1 pkg low-fat pastry crust mix
  for a 10-inch single-crust
  pie

1. Preheat the oven to 375 degrees. Heat the chicken broth
   to a simmer, add the seafood, and cook for 5–10 minutes.
   Remove the seafood from the broth and reserve the broth.
2. Heat the oil in a skillet over medium heat and saute the
   onions and celery until tender. Stir in the flour, add the
   reserved broth, and cook, stirring frequently, until
   thickened. Add the seafood, sherry, and pepper. Stir, then
   allow to cool.
3. Pour the mixture into a nonstick casserole dish and top
   with the pastry. Cut vents in top so that steam can escape.
   Bake for 25–30 minutes or until the pastry is golden brown.

Starch Exchange 1
Very Lean Meat Exchange 1
Fat Exchange 1
Calories 160
  Calories from Fat 83
Total Fat ....9 g
  Saturated Fat ....3 g

Cholesterol ....19 mg
Sodium ....216 mg
Carbohydrate......................14 g
  Dietary Fiber ....1 g
  Sugars................................1 g
Protein................................7 g

Shrimp Fried Rice

8 servings/serving size: 1½ cups
Preparation time: 15 minutes

Using a rice steamer helps keep rice from getting gummy. Try using brown rice for the most nutrition. Cook the rice the day before, if you can, so it will be as dry as possible.

¼ cup sesame oil
2 cloves garlic, minced
1½ cups chopped celery
1½ cups chopped onion
¾ cup chopped bell pepper
1 lb peeled, deveined shrimp

2 cups cold, cooked rice
2 Tbsp lite soy sauce
1 Tbsp Worcestershire sauce
Fresh ground pepper to taste
Dash hot pepper sauce

1. Heat the oil in a large skillet or wok over medium-high heat and saute the garlic, celery, onion, and bell pepper for 3–4 minutes.
2. Add the remaining ingredients and cook for 3–4 more minutes, until the rice is hot and the shrimp turns pink.

Starch Exchange 1
Very Lean Meat Exchange 1
Fat Exchange 1
Calories 169
  Calories from Fat 66
Total Fat ....7 g
  Saturated Fat ....1 g
Cholesterol ....81 mg
Sodium ....384 mg
Carbohydrate ....15 g
  Dietary Fiber ....1 g
  Sugars.................................2 g
Protein.................................10 g

Shrimp Perleau

6 servings/serving size: 1 cup
Preparation time: 10 minutes

You can also bake this dish at 350 degrees for 1½–2 hours.

1 Tbsp olive oil
¾ cup chopped onion
¾ cup chopped celery
¾ cup chopped bell pepper
1 cup rice
1 Tbsp lite soy sauce
2½ cups canned tomatoes
  with juice

2 cups water
1 small clove garlic
1 Tbsp Worcestershire sauce
1½ lb peeled, deveined
  shrimp
3 slices bacon, cooked extra-
  crisp and drained
  thoroughly

1. Heat the oil in a large saucepan. Saute the onion, celery, and bell pepper until tender.
2. Add the remaining ingredients except the bacon, bring to boil, then lower heat and let simmer for 1½–2 hours. Crumble the bacon on top before serving.

Starch Exchange 2
Vegetable Exchange................1
Lean Meat Exchange..............2
Monounsaturated Fat
  Exchange...........................½
Calories 311
  Calories from Fat...............92

Total Fat..............................10 g
  Saturated Fat......................3 g
Cholesterol...................152 mg
Sodium ....556 mg
Carbohydrate.....................34 g
  Dietary Fiber ....2 g
  Sugars................................5 g
Protein................................20 g

83

Southern Fried Chicken

6 servings/serving size: 3 oz
Preparation time: 15 minutes

This is a healthier way to serve an old favorite!

**18 oz boneless, skinless
  chicken breast
2 cups low-fat buttermilk
½ cup crushed cornflakes**

**½ cup flour
¼ tsp salt
1 tsp pepper
3 Tbsp canola oil**

1. Soak the chicken in the buttermilk for 4–24 hours in the refrigerator. Discard the buttermilk. Combine the cornflakes, flour, salt, and pepper in a medium bowl.
2. Dredge the chicken in the mixture until completely coated. Heat the oil in a large skillet. Fry the chicken for 15–20 minutes, turning once. Drain on paper towels before serving.

Starch Exchange..................2½
Lean Meat Exchange..............2
Monounsaturated Fat
  Exchange...........................½
Calories 331
  Calories from Fat................88
Total Fat..............................10 g
  Saturated Fat......................1 g

Cholesterol......................53 mg
Sodium ....485 mg
Carbohydrate.....................35 g
  Dietary Fiber ....1 g
  Sugars................................5 g
Protein................................24 g

Spicy Sloppy Joes

6 servings/serving size: ⅙ recipe
Preparation time: 5 minutes

Try serving this recipe over rice instead of hamburger buns for a change of pace.

1 lb lean ground beef
½ cup chopped onion
½ cup chopped mushrooms
1 Tbsp catsup

1 tsp mustard
1 Tbsp vinegar
¼ tsp pepper
1 15-oz can tomato puree

Cook the ground beef and onion until the meat is browned. Drain off excess fat, add the remaining ingredients, and simmer 10–15 minutes.

Starch Exchange.....................½
Medium-Fat Meat
    Exchange...........................2
Calories 190
    Calories from Fat.................92
Total Fat..............................10 g
    Saturated Fat......................4 g

Cholesterol.......................47 mg
Sodium ....202 mg
Carbohydrate......................10 g
    Dietary Fiber.......................2 g
    Sugars.................................6 g
Protein................................15 g

Stuffed Baked Shrimp

6 servings/serving size: ⅙ recipe
Preparation time: 20 minutes

Buy the freshest shrimp possible for this recipe.

1 Tbsp olive oil
1 onion, chopped fine
¼ cup chopped bell pepper
½ lb crab meat
4 slices whole-wheat bread,
  crusts removed and cubed
2 Tbsp lite mayonnaise

½ tsp hot pepper sauce
½ tsp salt
1 tsp Worcestershire sauce
1 tsp mustard
¾ lb large or jumbo shrimp,
  butterflied (leave tails on)

1. Preheat the oven to 400 degrees. Heat the oil in a medium skillet and saute the onion and bell pepper until tender. Add the remaining ingredients and mix well.
2. Stuff each shrimp with a portion of the mixture. Place the shrimp in a nonstick baking dish and bake until golden brown, about 18 minutes.

Starch Exchange...................½	Cholesterol....................118 mg
Lean Meat Exchange..............2	Sodium ....509 mg
Calories 158	Carbohydrate........................9 g
Calories from Fat................49	Dietary Fiber ....1 g
Total Fat ....5 g	Sugars...................................2 g
Saturated Fat......................1 g	Protein................................17 g

Venison Chili

10 servings/serving size: $1\frac{1}{4}$ cups
Preparation time: 20 minutes

This recipe is relatively high in sodium.

4 slices bacon, cut into $\frac{1}{2}$ inch pieces
2 Tbsp olive oil
1 large onion, chopped
1 cup chopped bell pepper
1 cup chopped celery
$1\frac{1}{2}$ lb ground venison
1 16-oz can kidney beans, undrained

3 cups water
1 28-oz can chopped tomatoes, undrained
1 Tbsp chili powder
1 tsp pepper
1 tsp salt
1 tsp cumin
1 tsp garlic powder

1. Cook the bacon in a large skillet until crisp; drain well and discard the drippings. Heat the oil and saute the onion, bell pepper, and celery for 3–4 minutes. Add the venison and cook over medium heat until meat is browned, stirring to crumble.
2. Transfer the venison, bacon, and all remaining ingredients to a large stockpot and bring to a boil. Cover, reduce heat, and simmer for $1\frac{1}{2}$ hours, stirring occasionally.

Starch Exchange 1
Lean Meat Exchange..............2
Calories 186
  Calories from Fat..............55
Total Fat ....6 g
  Saturated Fat...................1 g

Cholesterol......................59 mg
Sodium ....598 mg
Carbohydrate.....................14 g
  Dietary Fiber ....3 g
  Sugars................................5 g
Protein...............................20 g

Vegetables & Side Dishes

Baked Acorn Squash
Baked Beets
Charleston Gumbo
Cheese Grits Souffle
Cheese Grits with Turnip Greens
Corn Pudding
Creamed Spinach
Creole Peas and Okra
Down-Home Beans and Potatoes
Hoppin' John
Jerusalem Artichokes and Lima Beans
Jerusalem Artichokes with Parsley
Mashed Rutabagas
Oven-Fried Green Tomatoes
Pickled Beets
Ratatouille
Red Cabbage
Red Rice
Seasoned Collard or Mustard Greens
Southern Succotash
Spicy Baked Beans
Squash Casserole
Sweet Potato Crisps
Sweet Potato Pone
Sweet Potato Souffle
Swiss Chard with Tomatoes
Wild Rice with Fruit and Almonds

Baked Acorn Squash

4 servings/serving size: ½ squash
Preparation time: 10 minutes

Winter squash is so naturally sweet you could easily omit the maple syrup in this recipe.

2 medium acorn squash
1 Tbsp lemon juice
2 tsp corn oil
4 tsp pure maple syrup

Dash allspice (or other spice of choice)
2 Tbsp chopped walnuts

1. Preheat the oven to 400 degrees. Cut each squash in half and scoop out the seeds. Place the squash cut side down in a nonstick baking dish. Bake for 30–40 minutes or until tender.
2. Turn the squash cut side up and drizzle with lemon juice. Fill each half with ½ tsp oil, 1 tsp maple syrup, allspice, and ½ Tbsp walnuts. Return to the oven and bake 5 more minutes.

Starch Exchange 1
Polyunsaturated Fat
   Exchange...........................1
Calories 114
   Calories from Fat................44
Total Fat ....5 g
   Saturated Fat......................1 g
Cholesterol.........................0 mg
Sodium ....6 mg
Carbohydrate.....................18 g
   Dietary Fiber ....4 g
   Sugars................................9 g
Protein..................................1 g

Baked Beets

4 servings/serving size: 1 beet
Preparation time: 10 minutes

If you hate beets, you probably have never tried fresh baked beets. The taste is unbelievable. And don't throw those beet greens away—use them in salads, or saute them in a small amount of olive or sesame oil and top with sesame seeds.

4 6-oz beets   **2 tsp olive oil**
1 clove garlic, minced   **Fresh ground pepper to taste**

1. Preheat the oven to 400 degrees. Wash the beets and cut the stems to within 2 inches of the bulb. Place the beets in a baking pan and bake 50–60 minutes until tender.
2. Slice off the top and root end so the beets can stand on a plate. With a fork, mash down on the center part of the beet. Sprinkle with garlic, olive oil, and pepper.

Vegetable Exchange.................2	Cholesterol.......................0 mg
Monounsaturated Fat	Sodium ....82 mg
Exchange ....½	Carbohydrate.....................11 g
Calories 67	Dietary Fiber ....2 g
Calories from Fat.................23	Sugars.................................6 g
Total Fat ....3 g	Protein.................................2 g
Saturated Fat.....................0 g	

Charleston Gumbo

6 servings/serving size: ¾ cup
Preparation time: 15 minutes

Traditional Southern farmers beat their okra with a stick to make it grow better. Try it: take a small branch and lightly smack each plant.

2 slices of bacon, diced
1 cup white onion, chopped
4 cups okra, sliced
1 32-oz can tomatoes or 4
  medium fresh tomatoes

Fresh ground pepper to taste
Dash Worcestershire sauce

Fry the bacon and onion in a medium saucepan until browned. Drain off the fat, then add the remaining ingredients and simmer for 1–2 hours.

Vegetable Exchange................3
Calories 81
  Calories from Fat................14
Total Fat ....2 g
  Saturated Fat.....................0 g
Cholesterol.......................2 mg

Sodium ....286 mg
Carbohydrate.....................15 g
  Dietary Fiber ....4 g
  Sugars................................7 g
Protein................................4 g

Cheese Grits Souffle

6 servings/serving size: ⅔ cup
Preparation time: 25 minutes

This is a great way to dress up a classic Southern favorite.

1 small onion, chopped
1 medium bell pepper,
    chopped
1½ cups skim milk
1 cup water
½ cup grits
½ tsp baking powder
1 Tbsp butter, melted

½ tsp sugar
2 eggs, separated
½ cup low-fat, sharp cheddar
    cheese
⅓ cup unprocessed,
    uncooked wheat bran
Dash hot pepper sauce

1. Preheat the oven to 375 degrees. Saute the onion and bell pepper in a nonstick pan until browned. Set aside. In a large saucepan, heat the milk to scalding; add the water and the grits and cook until thick, stirring constantly.
2. Add the baking powder, butter, and sugar; mix well. Beat the egg yolks and add to grits. Add the cheese and hot pepper sauce. Whip the egg whites until they form soft peaks; fold in. Pour the souffle into a 1½-quart, nonstick casserole or souffle dish. Bake for 30 minutes. Serve hot.

Starch Exchange..................1½
Saturated Fat Exchange 1
Calories 173
    Calories from Fat...............65
Total Fat..................................7 g
    Saturated Fat......................4 g

Cholesterol......................87 mg
Sodium ....162 mg
Carbohydrate......................20 g
    Dietary Fiber ....2 g
    Sugars.................................5 g
Protein....................................9 g

Cheese Grits with Turnip Greens

8 servings/serving size: ¾ cup
Preparation time: 20 minutes

To "rough up" grits, add 2–4 Tbsp unprocessed, uncooked wheat bran and 1 Tbsp water to every ¼ cup dry grits. This will increase the volume and the fiber content of the grits without changing the flavor significantly.

3 cups water
½ tsp salt
1 cup grits
1 Tbsp olive oil
2 large cloves garlic, minced
4 cups frozen chopped turnip
  greens (about 15–16 oz),
  thawed and squeezed dry
  (or 1 bunch fresh greens,
  chopped)

1 cup packed, grated, low-fat,
  sharp cheddar cheese
  (about 5 oz)
Dash hot pepper sauce

1. Preheat the oven to 375 degrees. Bring the salted water to a boil in a medium saucepan. Gradually whisk the grits into the water.
2. Reduce the heat to low, cover, and cook until the grits are tender and the mixture is thick, stirring occasionally (about 8–10 minutes).
3. Meanwhile, heat the oil in a large skillet over medium heat. Add the garlic and saute for 1 minute. Add the greens and saute 2 more minutes.

4. Add the greens, ¾ cup of the cheese, and the hot pepper sauce to the grits. Transfer to a 1½-quart nonstick casserole or souffle dish. Sprinkle the remaining ¼ cup cheese on top. Bake until the cheese melts and the grits are heated through, about 15 minutes. Let stand 5 minutes before serving.

Starch Exchange	1	Total Fat	5 g
Vegetable Exchange	1	Saturated Fat	2 g
Very Lean Meat Exchange	1	Cholesterol	9 mg
Monounsaturated Fat		Sodium	256 mg
Exchange	½	Carbohydrate	21 g
Calories	165	Dietary Fiber	3 g
Calories from Fat	42	Sugars	1 g
		Protein	10 g

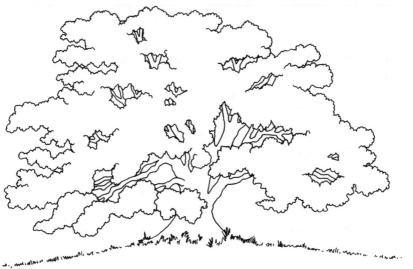

Corn Pudding

12 servings/serving size: ½ cup
Preparation time: 20 minutes

This recipe originated from Jamestown settlers many generations ago.

2 Tbsp corn oil
1 medium onion, chopped
2 Tbsp flour
2 eggs
3 cups fresh or frozen corn kernels (thawed)

1 cup skim milk
½ tsp salt
½ tsp nutmeg
1 Tbsp sugar

1. Position the rack in the center of the oven and preheat to 350 degrees. Heat the oil in a large skillet over medium heat. Add the onions and saute until very soft, about 12 minutes. Mix in the flour and cook, stirring, for 3–4 minutes.
2. Transfer the mixture to a bowl and cool to lukewarm. Add the eggs to the cooled mixture and whisk to blend. Mix in remaining ingredients.
3. Pour the pudding into the individual cups of a 6-cup nonstick souffle dish. Bake the puddings until a knife inserted into the center of each comes out clean, about 1 hour. Use a spoon to serve.

Starch Exchange 1
Polyunsaturated Fat
    Exchange ....½
Calories 89
    Calories from Fat 31
Total Fat ....3 g
    Saturated Fat ....1 g
Cholesterol ....36 mg
Sodium ....120 mg
Carbohydrate....................13 g
    Dietary Fiber ....1 g
    Sugars..........................4 g
Protein..............................3 g

Creamed Spinach

8 servings/serving size: $\frac{1}{2}$ cup
Preparation time: 10 minutes

This dish is a great complement to poached or broiled fish.

2 10-oz pkgs frozen, chopped
  spinach
1 can low-fat cream of
  chicken or mushroom
  soup, undiluted
1 clove garlic, minced

1 Tbsp flour
2 tsp grated onion
$\frac{1}{8}$ tsp salt
$\frac{1}{4}$ tsp pepper
1 hard-cooked egg, sliced

1. Preheat the oven to 375 degrees. Cook the spinach according to package directions; drain well.
2. Add the remaining ingredients except the egg; spoon into a 1$\frac{1}{2}$-quart nonstick casserole dish.
3. Bake for 15 minutes. Garnish with sliced egg before serving.

Vegetable Exchange	1
Fat Exchange	$\frac{1}{2}$
Calories	50
Calories from Fat	16
Total Fat	2 g
Saturated Fat	0 g
Cholesterol	28 mg
Sodium	339 mg
Carbohydrate	7 g
Dietary Fiber	2 g
Sugars	1 g
Protein	3 g

Creole Peas and Okra

10 servings/serving size: 1 cup
Preparation time: 10 minutes

You can also add other light vegetables, such as yellow squash or zucchini, to this dish.

2 Tbsp corn oil
1 cup diced celery
1 cup diced bell pepper
1 cup diced onion
2 medium hot peppers, chopped
2 16-oz cans chopped tomatoes with juice

3 cups cooked black-eyed peas with juice
2 10-oz pkgs frozen cut okra, partially thawed, or 1 lb fresh okra, sliced
½ tsp salt

1. Heat the oil in a medium skillet and saute the celery, bell pepper, onion, and hot pepper until tender.
2. Add the remaining ingredients and bring to a boil. Lower heat and simmer until okra is tender, about 15 minutes.

Starch Exchange 1
Vegetable Exchange...............1
Polyunsaturated Fat
     Exchange ....½
Calories 138
     Calories from Fat...............35
Total Fat ....4 g
     Saturated Fat.....................1 g

Cholesterol........................0 mg
Sodium ....379 mg
Carbohydrate....................22 g
     Dietary Fiber ....6 g
     Sugars................................8 g
Protein...............................6 g

Down-Home Beans and Potatoes

6 servings/serving size: 1 cup
Preparation time: 10 minutes

This dish tastes just as good with 1 Tbsp olive oil substituted for the bacon.

1½ lb fresh green beans
2 slices bacon, chopped
1 small onion, chopped

5 cups water
½ tsp pepper
1½ cups cubed red potatoes

1. Wash the beans and trim the ends. Cut the beans into 1½-inch pieces. Fry the bacon until crisp; drain well and discard the drippings. Saute the onion in the same pan until tender.
2. Add the water to the onion and bring to a boil. Add the bacon, beans, pepper, and potatoes and return to a boil. Cover and simmer 15 minutes or until the vegetables are tender.

Starch Exchange.....................½	Cholesterol.........................2 mg
Vegetable Exchange................2	Sodium ....38 mg
Calories 85	Carbohydrate......................16 g
Calories from Fat................12	Dietary Fiber ....4 g
Total Fat ....1 g	Sugars.....................................3 g
Saturated Fat..................0 mg	Protein....................................4 g

99

Hoppin' John

8 servings/serving size: ¾ cup
Preparation time: 10 minutes

A Southern favorite on New Year's Day, this dish is said to bring good luck. Add a pot of greens to ensure prosperity!

1 tsp canola oil
1 cup chopped onion
1 cup chopped celery
3½ cups water
1 cup dried field peas or
    black-eyed peas

1 cup uncooked brown rice
4 slices bacon, fried crisp and
    fat drained, chopped

1. Heat the oil in a skillet and saute the onion and celery for 3–4 minutes.
2. Bring the water to boil in a saucepan; add the peas, onion, and celery and cook until the peas are tender, about 60 minutes.
3. Add the rice and bacon and cook for 1 hour or until the rice is thoroughly done.

Starch Exchange 2	Cholesterol.......................3 mg
Fat Exchange ....½	Sodium ....70 mg
Calories 192	Carbohydrate....................34 g
Calories from Fat.................28	Dietary Fiber ....4 g
Total Fat.................................3 g	Sugars.................................3 g
Saturated Fat......................1 g	Protein.................................8 g

Jerusalem Artichokes and Lima Beans

6 servings/serving size: ⅔ cup
Preparation time: 10 minutes

Jerusalem artichokes are high in fiber and have an interesting taste and texture.

1 Tbsp canola oil
1 lb Jerusalem artichokes, scrubbed, quartered lengthwise, and chopped

2 red bell peppers, chopped
1 10-oz pkg frozen baby lima beans, thawed
¾ cup water

1. Heat the oil in a skillet over medium heat and saute the artichokes for 5 minutes.
2. Add the remaining ingredients, cover, and cook until the limas are tender, stirring occasionally, about 15 minutes.

Starch Exchange..................1½
Monounsaturated Fat
   Exchange..........................½
Calories.................................142
   Calories from Fat...............23
Total Fat.................................3 g
   Saturated Fat.....................0 g

Cholesterol.........................0 mg
Sodium..............................31 mg
Carbohydrate.......................26 g
   Dietary Fiber......................5 g
   Sugars................................6 g
Protein...................................5 g

Jerusalem Artichokes with Parsley

4 servings/serving size: 1 cup
Preparation time: 10 minutes

This simple recipe is great with broiled chicken or fish.

1 Tbsp olive oil
1 small onion, chopped
1 lb Jerusalem artichokes,
  peeled and thinly sliced

1 tsp cider vinegar
Dash cayenne pepper
2 Tbsp chopped parsley

1. Heat the oil in a medium skillet and saute the onion until tender.
2. Add the artichokes, vinegar, and pepper and cook until the artichokes are lightly browned, stirring constantly. Sprinkle with parsley and serve.

Starch Exchange..................1½
Calories 124
  Calories from Fat...............31
Total Fat ....3 g
  Saturated Fat.....................0 g
Cholesterol.......................0 mg

Sodium ....6 mg
Carbohydrate.....................22 g
  Dietary Fiber ....2 g
Sugars..................................7 g
Protein..................................3 g

Mashed Rutabagas

8 servings/serving size: $\frac{1}{2}$ cup
Preparation time: 10 minutes

Try this recipe instead of mashed potatoes. The carbohydrate content is lower and you get plenty of vitamins and minerals.

**$2\frac{1}{4}$ lb rutabagas, peeled and
    sliced in $\frac{1}{2}$-inch slices**
**$\frac{1}{2}$ cup low-fat, low-sodium
    chicken broth, hot**

1 Tbsp honey
$\frac{1}{4}$ tsp allspice
$\frac{1}{4}$ tsp nutmeg
Dash cayenne pepper

Boil the rutabagas in unsalted water 30–40 minutes or until tender. Drain and mash the rutabagas with a potato masher. Add the remaining ingredients and mix well.

Vegetable Exchange................2	Sodium ....210 mg
Calories 48	Carbohydrate......................10 g
Calories from Fat 6	Dietary Fiber ....2 g
Total Fat ....1 g	Sugars..................................7 g
Saturated Fat ....0 g	Protein..................................2 g
Cholesterol ....0 mg	

Oven-Fried Green Tomatoes

6 servings/serving size: ⅙ recipe
Preparation time: 10 minutes

This is a great version of a Southern favorite!

¼ cup stone-ground
  cornmeal
3 Tbsp unprocessed,
  uncooked wheat bran
¼ tsp salt
¼ tsp pepper

1 egg, well-beaten, mixed
  with 1 Tbsp water
1 Tbsp canola oil
2 large green tomatoes, cut
  into ½-inch slices

1. Preheat the oven to 450 degrees. Combine the cornmeal, bran, salt, and pepper. In a separate bowl, mix the egg and the oil.
2. Dip the tomatoes in the egg mixture, then into the cornmeal mixture. Place the coated tomato slices on a nonstick cookie sheet and bake for 35–40 minutes until golden brown.

Starch Exchange..................½	Cholesterol......................35 mg
Monounsaturated Fat	Sodium ....114 mg
Exchange ....½	Carbohydrate......................9 g
Calories 72	Dietary Fiber ....2 g
Calories from Fat...............32	Sugars...................................2 g
Total Fat ....4 g	Protein.................................2 g
Saturated Fat.....................0 g	

Pickled Beets

5 servings/serving size: ½ cup
Preparation time: 5 minutes

This pretty dish goes well with chilled turkey. Serve on ruffled lettuce leaves.

**2½ cups cooked or canned
  beets, sliced (reserve ¾
  cup liquid)
⅓ cup cider vinegar**

**½ tsp salt
4 whole cloves
1 bay leaf
1 Tbsp sugar**

1. Drain the liquid from the beets into a saucepan; add the remaining ingredients and bring to a boil.
2. Pour the liquid over the beets and chill about 4 hours before serving. Serve cold or reheat.

Vegetable Exchange................2
Calories 49
  Calories from Fat 2
Total Fat ....0 g
  Saturated Fat ....0 g
Cholesterol ....0 mg

Sodium ....298 mg
Carbohydrate....................12 g
  Dietary Fiber ....1 g
  Sugars................................8 g
Protein................................1 g

Ratatouille

6 servings/serving size: 1 cup
Preparation time: 10 minutes

Ratatouille is great made with fresh vegetables from your garden.

1 Tbsp olive oil
1 cup chopped onion
$^{2}/_{3}$ cup finely chopped bell
   pepper
1 clove garlic, chopped
1$^{1}/_{2}$ lb eggplant, peeled
   and cut in $^{1}/_{2}$-inch cubes
1 lb zucchini, unpeeled
   and cut in $^{1}/_{2}$-inch slices

1 tsp basil
1 tsp marjoram
3 medium tomatoes, peeled
   and quartered
$^{1}/_{2}$ tsp salt
$^{1}/_{4}$ tsp pepper
2 Tbsp Parmesan cheese

1. Heat the oil in a large skillet and saute the onion, bell pepper, and garlic for 3–4 minutes.
2. Add all remaining ingredients except the Parmesan cheese, cover, and cook over medium heat, stirring occasionally, for about 10 minutes or until vegetables are tender-crisp. Garnish with cheese to serve.

Vegetable Exchange................3	Cholesterol.........................1 mg
Monounsaturated Fat	Sodium ....237 mg
Exchange ....$^{1}/_{2}$	Carbohydrate......................16 g
Calories 94	Dietary Fiber ....4 g
Calories from Fat................29	Sugars..................................9 g
Total Fat ....3 g	Protein....................................3 g
Saturated Fat......................1 g	

Red Cabbage

10 servings/serving size: ½ cup
Preparation time: 10 minutes

A nice complement to pork tenderloin, red cabbage provides a burst of color and nutrition.

1 medium red cabbage, sliced fine
1 large apple, peeled and sliced
¾ cup vinegar
½ cup water
Dash salt
Fresh ground pepper to taste

Cook all ingredients together in a covered saucepan until the cabbage is tender, about 30 minutes.

Vegetable Exchange................2
Calories 40
   Calories from Fat 5
Total Fat ....1 g
   Saturated Fat......................0 g
Cholesterol........................0 mg
Sodium ....10 mg
Carbohydrate.....................10 g
   Dietary Fiber ....4 g
   Sugars................................6 g
Protein.................................1 g

Red Rice

6 servings/serving size: ⅔ cup
Preparation time: 10 minutes

You can use lean ground turkey instead of bacon in this
recipe if you prefer.

4 slices bacon
1 large onion, chopped (or 2 small)
¾ cup chopped celery
¾ cup chopped bell pepper
1 cup uncooked long-grain or brown rice

1 16-oz can chopped whole tomatoes, undrained
½ cup water
½ tsp salt
¼ tsp pepper
¼ tsp cayenne pepper
⅛ tsp hot pepper sauce

1. Preheat the oven to 350 degrees. Cook the bacon in a
   skillet until crisp. Remove the bacon, drain well, crumble,
   and set aside. Discard the excess bacon drippings, leaving
   only a thin film coating the skillet.
2. Add the onion, celery, and bell pepper to the pan and
   saute until the vegetables are tender. Stir in the remaining
   ingredients. Spray a 1½-quart baking dish lightly with
   nonstick cooking spray and add the rice. Bake, covered, for
   40 minutes or until rice is tender, stirring after 15 minutes.

Starch Exchange 2
Vegetable Exchange 1
Calories 170
   Calories from Fat 22
Total Fat ....2 g
   Saturated Fat ....1 g

Cholesterol ....3 mg
Sodium ....368 mg
Carbohydrate ....32 g
   Dietary Fiber ....2 g
   Sugars ....4 g
Protein ....5 g

Seasoned Collard or Mustard Greens

4 servings/serving size: ½ cup
Preparation time: 10 minutes

Traditional Southern greens are flavored with animal fat. A newer way to prepare greens is to saute them in a small amount of sesame oil or broth, top with toasted sesame seeds, and serve with a dash of lite soy sauce on the side.

**1 bunch fresh collard or
mustard greens or 1 1-lb
pkg frozen greens
2 cups boiling water**

**½ tsp salt
1 slice bacon, chopped
Fresh ground pepper to taste**

1. If using fresh greens, wash them thoroughly, cut the stems away from the leaves, and chop stems and leaves into bite-size pieces. If using frozen greens, defrost them.
2. Place fresh or frozen greens in boiling water. Add the salt and bacon and simmer, uncovered, over low heat for 30 minutes. Drain the greens well and sprinkle with pepper to serve.

Vegetable Exchange................1
Fat Exchange ....½
Calories 44
   Calories from Fat................10
Total Fat..............................1 g
   Saturated Fat.....................0 g

Cholesterol.........................1 mg
Sodium ....364 mg
Carbohydrate.......................7 g
   Dietary Fiber.....................2 g
   Sugars................................0 g
Protein.................................3 g

Southern Succotash

10 servings/serving size: ½ cup
Preparation time: 5 minutes

There are many variations of this recipe, but the most basic consists of lima beans and corn. This variation is a little bit lighter and quite tasty.

1 cup frozen lima beans
1 lb fresh or frozen green beans

3 large tomatoes, peeled
1 cup frozen corn kernels
2 Tbsp canola oil

1. Cook the lima and green beans with the tomatoes in boiling water until the beans are tender, about 15 minutes.
2. Add the corn and cook until done, about 5 minutes. Toss lightly with oil to serve.

Starch Exchange......................½
Vegetable Exchange................1
Monounsaturated Fat
   Exchange...........................½
Calories 87
   Calories from Fat.................29
Total Fat ....3 g
   Saturated Fat.......................0 g

Cholesterol.........................0 mg
Sodium ....20 mg
Carbohydrate......................13 g
   Dietary Fiber ....4 g
   Sugars..................................3 g
Protein...................................3 g

Spicy Baked Beans

10 servings/serving size: ⅓ cup
Preparation time: 10 minutes

Even low-fat baked beans are still very high in calories. Try
using demitasse cups (or very small individual casserole
dishes) to help with portion control.

2 cups dry navy beans
½ cup chili sauce
1 tsp vinegar
1 medium onion, sliced

¼ lb lean boneless pork, cut
in small cubes
1 tsp dry mustard
¼ cup dark molasses or
sorghum

1. Rinse and sort the beans. Cover with water to a 2-inch level
   above the beans and soak overnight.
2. The next day, drain the beans and add fresh water to a 2-
   inch level above the beans. Add the pork, cover, and
   simmer over low heat (do not boil) until just tender, about
   1 hour. Drain, reserving 2 cups of the bean liquid.
3. Preheat the oven to 300 degrees. Pour the beans into a 2-
   quart casserole dish. Combine the remaining ingredients
   and add to the beans. Mix well, then cover and bake for 4
   hours. If necessary, add the bean liquid during cooking to
   thin.

Starch Exchange..................2½
Calories 195
  Calories from Fat...............10
Total Fat...............................1 g
  Saturated Fat......................0 g
Cholesterol.......................7 mg

Sodium ....177 mg
Carbohydrate.....................35 g
  Dietary Fiber...................10 g
  Sugars...............................9 g
Protein...............................12 g

Squash Casserole

8 servings/serving size: ½ cup
Preparation time: 10 minutes

This colorful dish is great with roast chicken.

1 Tbsp canola oil
1 medium onion, chopped
1 lb yellow squash, sliced
1 cup shredded carrots
1 6-oz pkg stuffing mix
1 cup lite sour cream

1 egg
1 cup low-fat, low-sodium
   chicken broth (or enough
   to moisten)
Nonstick cooking spray

1. Preheat the oven to 375 degrees. Heat the oil in a small
   skillet over medium heat. Add the onion and saute for 5
   minutes.
2. Combine the remaining ingredients in a large bowl, add
   the onion, and mix well. Spray a 2-quart baking dish with
   nonstick cooking spray and transfer the mixture to the
   dish. Bake for 30–40 minutes or until bubbly.

Starch Exchange 1	Cholesterol.......................37 mg
Vegetable Exchange................1	Sodium ....356 mg
Fat Exchange 1	Carbohydrate......................23 g
Calories 163	Dietary Fiber ....3 g
Calories from Fat................54	Sugars..................................5 g
Total Fat ....6 g	Protein..................................5 g
Saturated Fat......................2 g	

Sweet Potato Crisps

4 servings/serving size: ½ potato
Preparation time: 5 minutes

Try snacking on this healthy Southern variation of a national favorite!

**2 medium sweet potatoes,
  peeled and sliced ½-inch
  thick (the long way)**

**1 tsp salt
Olive oil-flavored nonstick
  cooking spray**

1. Preheat the oven to 375 degrees. Drop the sweet potatoes into a bowl with enough cold water to cover. Add the salt and soak for 5 minutes. Dry the potatoes.
2. Spray a baking pan with nonstick cooking spray, place the potato slices in the pan, and spray the potatoes on all sides. Bake for 20–25 minutes, turning once.

Starch Exchange 1
Calories 76
  Calories from Fat 1
Total Fat ....0 g
  Saturated Fat ....0 g
Cholesterol ....0 mg
Sodium ....589 mg
Carbohydrate.....................18 g
  Dietary Fiber ....2 g
  Sugars..................................8 g
Protein...................................1 g

Sweet Potato Pone

8 servings/serving size: ½ cup
Preparation time: 5 minutes

Serve this creamy casserole with grilled pork or beef.

3 large sweet potatoes,
  peeled and grated
2 Tbsp butter, melted
3 eggs, beaten
2 cups skim milk

1½ tsp vanilla
Zest of 1 whole orange
2 Tbsp sugar
Nonstick cooking spray

1. Preheat the oven to 350 degrees. Drizzle the butter over the sweet potatoes. Combine the remaining ingredients and stir into the potato mixture.
2. Spray a 2-quart casserole dish with nonstick cooking spray and add the potato mixture. Bake until firm and browned, about 1½ hours. Slice and serve hot or cold.

Starch Exchange 2
Saturated Fat Exchange........½
Calories 179
  Calories from Fat 46
Total Fat ....5 g
  Saturated Fat ....3 g
Cholesterol ....89 mg
Sodium ....96 mg
Carbohydrate.....................28 g
  Dietary Fiber ....3 g
  Sugars...............................14 g
Protein.................................6 g

Sweet Potato Souffle

6 servings/serving size: ⅓ cup
Preparation time: 5 minutes

This light sweet potato dish goes well with fresh fish or poultry.

1 Tbsp canola oil
½ cup skim milk
1 tsp cinnamon
½ tsp salt
1 egg

½ tsp orange zest
3 medium sweet potatoes,
**   baked and peeled**
Nonstick cooking spray
⅓ cup walnuts

1. Preheat the oven to 350 degrees. Add all ingredients except the walnuts and nonstick cooking spray to the sweet potatoes and beat until smooth.
2. Spray a 1½-quart casserole dish with nonstick cooking spray and add the sweet potato mixture. Top with walnuts and bake for 20–30 minutes or until bubbly.

Starch Exchange...................1½	Cholesterol......................36 mg
Fat Exchange 1	Sodium ....223 mg
Calories 156	Carbohydrate.....................20 g
Calories from Fat................64	Dietary Fiber ....3 g
Total Fat...................................7 g	Sugars.................................10 g
Saturated Fat......................1 g	Protein..................................4 g

Swiss Chard
with Tomatoes

6 servings/serving size: ⅔ cup
Preparation time: 10 minutes

You'll love this colorful, nutritious dish.

2 lb Swiss chard
1 Tbsp olive oil
2 cloves garlic, minced

1½ cups fresh peeled and
chopped tomatoes
Fresh ground pepper to taste

1. Wash the chard thoroughly and drain well. Remove the leaves from the stalks and cut both stalks and leaves into 1-inch pieces.
2. Cook the chard, covered, in 1 inch of boiling water for 3–5 minutes or until tender. Drain and set aside. Heat the oil in a large skillet over medium heat, add the garlic, and saute until golden.
3. Add the tomatoes and pepper to the skillet, cover, and simmer 8–10 minutes. Add the chard and cook, uncovered, for 10 minutes, stirring frequently.

Vegetable Exchange................1
Monounsaturated Fat
    Exchange..........................½
Calories 57
    Calories from Fat...............23
Total Fat..............................3 g
    Saturated Fat......................0 g

Cholesterol.........................0 mg
Sodium ....230 mg
Carbohydrate.......................8 g
    Dietary Fiber.....................3 g
    Sugars...............................2 g
Protein................................3 g

Wild Rice with Fruit and Almonds

6 servings/serving size: ⅔ cup
Preparation time: 10 minutes

You'll enjoy the texture of this nutritious side dish. You can find walnut oil in gourmet sections of grocery stores.

⅔ cup wild rice
½ cup chopped celery
1½ cups low-fat, low-sodium chicken broth
1 Tbsp walnut oil

½ cup chopped Red Delicious apple
¼ cup currants
2 Tbsp chopped parsley
3 Tbsp toasted almonds

1. Combine the rice, celery, chicken broth, and oil in a medium saucepan. Bring to a boil, cover, reduce heat, and simmer 25–30 minutes or until the rice is tender.
2. Remove from heat and stir in the apple, currants, and parsley. Mix gently and sprinkle with toasted almonds to serve.

Starch Exchange 1	Cholesterol ....0 mg
Fat Exchange ....½	Sodium ....29 mg
Calories 113	Carbohydrate.....................17 g
Calories from Fat................39	Dietary Fiber ....2 g
Total Fat................................4 g	Sugars.................................2 g
Saturated Fat......................1 g	Protein................................4 g

Sauces, Gravies, & Dressings

Anytime Cranberry Relish
Best Barbecue Sauce
Celery Seed Dressing
Classic Herb Vinaigrette
Lemon Marinade
Low-Fat Giblet Gravy
Perfect Pesto
Seafood Herb Dressing
Sesame Dressing
Spicy Vinegar

Anytime Cranberry Relish

12 servings/serving size: ¼ cup
Preparation time: 5 minutes

This light relish is good with roast turkey, chicken, ham, or pork. Buy frozen cranberries if you can't find fresh.

1 orange, peeled, quartered, and seeds removed
2 cups fresh cranberries
1 cup diced, unpeeled apple

1 8-oz can crushed, unsweetened pineapple, drained
3 Tbsp sugar

1. Place the orange in a blender or food processor and process until coarsely ground. Spoon into a medium bowl and set aside.
2. Repeat with the cranberries. Combine all ingredients in a medium bowl and mix well. Cover and chill 8 hours.

Fruit Exchange .... ½
Calories 37
  Calories from Fat 1
Total Fat .... 0 g
  Saturated Fat .... 0 g
Cholesterol .... 0 mg
Sodium .... 1 mg
Carbohydrate .... 10 g
  Dietary Fiber .... 1 g
Sugars .... 8 g
Protein .... 0 g

Best Barbecue Sauce

32 servings/serving size: 2 Tbsp
Preparation time: 10 minutes

Barbecue sauce tastes great on anything from chicken to tofu!

2 Tbsp peanut oil
2 cloves garlic, minced
1 large yellow onion, diced
1 cup cider vinegar
¼ cup Dijon mustard
Dash hot pepper sauce
2 Tbsp molasses or brown
  sugar

½ cup water
1 tsp Worcestershire sauce
1 Tbsp dry mustard
1 Tbsp chili powder
Fresh ground pepper to taste
2 cups pureed tomatoes

1. Heat the oil in a large skillet over medium heat. Saute the garlic and onion until tender. Add the vinegar and simmer 15 minutes.
2. Add the next five ingredients and simmer 15 minutes. Add the dry mustard, chili powder, and pepper. Stir to blend thoroughly. Add the tomatoes and cook until thickened.

Vegetable Exchange................1
Calories 20
  Calories from Fat.................5
Total Fat...............................1 g
  Saturated Fat.....................0 g
Cholesterol.......................0 mg
Sodium ....61 mg
Carbohydrate......................4 g
  Dietary Fiber.....................1 g
  Sugars................................3 g
Protein.................................0 g

Celery Seed Dressing

10 servings/serving size: 2 Tbsp
Preparation time: 5 minutes

This dressing is great on spinach salad.

½ cup canola oil
¼ cup maple syrup
1 tsp dry mustard
½ tsp paprika

¼ cup cider vinegar
2 Tbsp lemon juice
1 tsp celery seed

Whisk together all ingredients except the celery seed. Stir in the celery seed. Chill before serving.

Carbohydrate Exchange ....½
Monounsaturated Fat
    Exchange...........................2
Calories 122
    Calories from Fat..............102
Total Fat..............................11 g
    Saturated Fat.......................1 g

Cholesterol........................0 mg
Sodium ....8 mg
Carbohydrate.........................6 g
    Dietary Fiber ....0 g
    Sugars...................................5 g
Protein..................................0 g

Classic Herb Vinaigrette

10 servings/serving size: 1 Tbsp
Preparation time: 5 minutes

You can also use this vinaigrette as a marinade for chicken or fish.

**3 Tbsp white wine or
  champagne vinegar
¼ cup chopped fresh herbs
  (try basil, dill, and thyme)**

**1 Tbsp lemon juice
¼ cup olive oil
Fresh ground pepper to taste**

Whisk together all ingredients and chill before serving.

Monounsaturated Fat Exchange............................1	Cholesterol.........................0 mg
Calories 49	Sodium ....0 mg
Calories from Fat.................49	Carbohydrate.......................0 g
Total Fat ....5 g	Dietary Fiber ....0 g
Saturated Fat.......................1 g	Sugars..................................0 g
	Protein..................................0 g

Lemon Marinade

6 servings/serving size: 2 Tbsp
Preparation time: 5 minutes

This is a quick, tasty way to marinate chicken or fish.

$^1\!/_2$ cup olive oil
Juice of 2 lemons
1 clove garlic, minced
$^1\!/_4$ cup dry white wine
3 tsp fresh rosemary (or 1$^1\!/_2$
   tsp ground)

Zest of 1 whole lemon
1 bay leaf, torn in half
Fresh ground white pepper
   to taste

Whisk all ingredients together in a bowl. Marinate chicken or fish for at least 30 minutes in the refrigerator before grilling.

Monounsaturated Fat Exchange	$^1\!/_2$	Cholesterol	0 mg
Calories	29	Sodium	2 mg
Calories from Fat	27	Carbohydrate	1 g
Total Fat	3 g	Dietary Fiber	0 g
Saturated Fat	0 g	Sugars	0 g
		Protein	0 g

Low-Fat Giblet Gravy

10 servings/serving size: ¼ cup
Preparation time: 15 minute

Southerners love giblet gravy. This low-fat version is great on holidays!

Giblets from turkey and turkey neck
2¼ cups low-fat, low-sodium chicken broth

1 Tbsp pan drippings from roast turkey
1 Tbsp flour
¼ tsp fresh ground pepper

1. Wash the giblets and neck and place in a saucepot with the chicken broth. Bring to a boil, then cover and cook over low heat for 45 minutes or until the giblets are tender. Drain the giblets, reserving broth. Chop giblets and as much meat from turkey neck as possible and set aside.
2. Measure 1 Tbsp of fat from the roasting pan into a small saucepot. Discard the remaining drippings. Add the giblet broth to the roasting pan and bring to a boil, scraping the bottom. Mix the flour into the fat in the saucepot and cook, stirring, until browned. Gradually add the liquid from the roasting pan and cook, stirring, until thickened. Add the chopped giblets and pepper and stir.

Medium-Fat Meat Exchange	1	Cholesterol	88 mg
Calories	80	Sodium	18 mg
Calories from Fat	41	Carbohydrate	1 g
Total Fat	5 g	Dietary Fiber	0 g
Saturated Fat	1 g	Sugars	0 g
		Protein	8 g

Perfect Pesto

14 servings/serving size: 2 Tbsp
Preparation time: 5 minutes

Pesto makes a marvelous alternative to butter or margarine. Use it as a topping for pasta, bread, or veggies. To make a lighter version of pesto, add 2 cups of finely chopped fresh spinach to this recipe.

1 cup fresh basil leaves, tightly packed
½ cup chopped parsley
¼ cup grated Parmesan cheese

¼ cup pine nuts or pecans
2 cloves garlic, peeled
¼ tsp salt
¼ cup olive oil

Process all ingredients except the oil in a blender or food processor until well blended. Add the oil gradually until the pesto is the desired consistency.

Monounsaturated Fat
    Exchange............................1
Calories 58
    Calories from Fat................52
Total Fat ....6 g
    Saturated Fat......................1 g

Cholesterol.........................1 mg
Sodium ....72 mg
Carbohydrate........................1 g
    Dietary Fiber ....0 g
    Sugars...................................0 g
Protein...................................2 g

Seafood Herb Dressing

6 servings/serving size: ¼ cup
Preparation time: 10 minutes

This dressing is great over any fresh seafood.

¾ cup plain nonfat yogurt
2 Tbsp any chopped fresh
   herbs
2 Tbsp lemon juice

¼ cup lite mayonnaise
½ cup finely chopped
   cucumber
Dash hot pepper sauce

Combine all ingredients and serve.

Polyunsaturated Fat
   Exchange.............................1
Calories 52
   Calories from Fat...............28
Total Fat.................................3 g
   Saturated Fat......................0 g

Cholesterol ....5 mg
Sodium ....100 mg
Carbohydrate.......................3 g
   Dietary Fiber ....0 g
   Sugars.................................3 g
Protein.................................2 g

Sesame Dressing

16 servings/serving size: 1 Tbsp
Preparation time: 5 minutes

Try this dressing over hot, steamed greens. To toast the sesame seeds, heat them in a dry skillet over low heat until they are light brown in color.

¼ cup canola oil
¼ cup rice vinegar
2 Tbsp dark sesame oil
1 Tbsp lite soy sauce
1 Tbsp toasted sesame seeds

1 Tbsp apple juice
1 tsp minced fresh ginger
   root or ½ tsp ground
   ginger
1 clove garlic, minced

Whisk all ingredients together.

Monounsaturated Fat Exchange...........1	Cholesterol.................0 mg
Calories 51	Sodium ....38 mg
Calories from Fat..........49	Carbohydrate.............1 g
Total Fat.............5 g	Dietary Fiber.............0 g
Saturated Fat.........1 g	Sugars.................1 g
	Protein.................0 g

Spicy Vinegar

64 servings/serving size: 2 Tbsp
Preparation time: 5 minutes

This tangy vinegar can be used in place of ordinary vinegar to perk up a great variety of recipes. Use it to thin down salad dressings, or add just a drop or two to dips and spreads for extra flavor.

8 cups cider vinegar
2 Tbsp whole pickling spice
4 peppercorns

4 Tbsp grated fresh ginger or
1 tsp ground ginger
$^1/_8$ tsp cayenne pepper

Combine all ingredients and boil for 15 minutes. Strain through several thicknesses of wet cheesecloth. Seal in hot, sterilized bottles until ready to use.

Free Food

Calories.....................................4	Sodium ....1 mg
Calories from Fat 0	Carbohydrate........................2 g
Total Fat ....0 g	Dietary Fiber ....0 g
Saturated Fat......................0 g	Sugars..................................2 g
Cholesterol........................0 mg	Protein..................................0 g

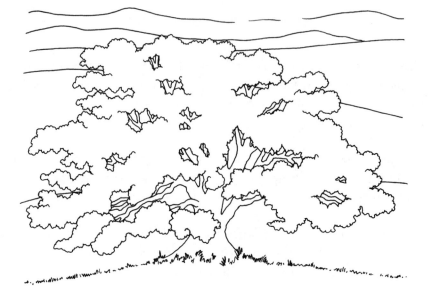

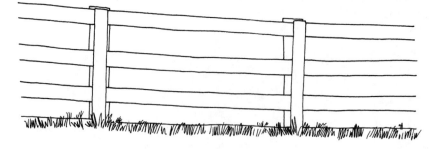

Breads

Banana-Nut Bread

Benne (Sesame) Seed Biscuits

Blueberry Buttermilk Muffins

Corn Bread Sticks

Corn Bread Stuffing

Crusty Corn Bread

Feather Rolls

Oven-Fried Hush Puppies

Pecan Waffles

Prune-Nut Bread

Spoon Bread

Sweet Potato Rolls

Whole-Wheat Soft Pretzels

Banana-Nut Bread

16 servings/serving size: one ½-inch-thick slice
Preparation time: 15 minutes

Try serving this sweet bread with chicken or shrimp salad.

2 cups whole-wheat flour
2 tsp baking powder
½ tsp baking soda
½ tsp nutmeg
2 eggs

2 Tbsp canola oil
¼ cup sugar
1½ cups sliced bananas
⅓ cup chopped pecans

1. Preheat the oven to 350 degrees. Combine the flour, baking powder, baking soda, and nutmeg in a mixing bowl. Process the eggs, oil, sugar, and bananas in a blender or food processor until smooth.
2. Pour the banana mixture into the flour and mix well. Add the pecans. Pour the batter into a nonstick 9 x 5-inch loaf pan. Bake for 40–50 minutes or until a toothpick inserted in the bread comes out clean. Remove from the oven and let cool for 5 minutes before removing from the pan.

Starch Exchange 1	Cholesterol......................27 mg
Fat Exchange ....½	Sodium ....94 mg
Calories 115	Carbohydrate....................18 g
Calories from Fat...............37	Dietary Fiber ....2 g
Total Fat................................4 g	Sugars..................................6 g
Saturated Fat.......................1 g	Protein.................................3 g

Benne (Sesame) Seed Biscuits

16 servings/serving size: 1 biscuit
Preparation time: 20 minutes

½ cup plus 1 Tbsp benne (sesame) seeds
2 cups flour
⅓ cup unprocessed, uncooked wheat bran

1 Tbsp baking powder
¾ tsp salt
¼ cup butter
¼ tsp baking soda
1 cup plain low-fat yogurt

1. Preheat the oven to 450 degrees. Place ½ cup sesame seeds in a medium skillet and brown over medium heat, stirring constantly.
2. Combine the dry ingredients in a large mixing bowl. Cut in the butter until the mixture resembles coarse cornmeal. Add the yogurt and stir well. Turn the dough out on a floured surface and knead lightly 10–12 times.
3. Roll out the dough to a ½-inch thickness; use additional bran, if necessary, to keep it from sticking. Cut with a 2-inch biscuit cutter. Sprinkle 1 Tbsp sesame seeds over the biscuit tops, pressing in slightly. Place the biscuits on a ungreased baking sheet and bake for 12–15 minutes.

Starch Exchange	1	Cholesterol	9 mg
Fat Exchange	1	Sodium	239 mg
Calories	126	Carbohydrate	16 g
Calories from Fat	54	Dietary Fiber	2 g
Total Fat	6 g	Sugars	2 g
Saturated Fat	2 g	Protein	4 g

Blueberry Buttermilk Muffins

18 servings/serving size: 1 muffin
Preparation time: 15 minutes

You can always freeze any leftover muffins for future use.

$1\frac{1}{2}$ cups flour
$\frac{1}{2}$ cup unprocessed,
   uncooked wheat bran
$\frac{1}{4}$ cup sugar
$2\frac{1}{4}$ tsp baking powder
1 tsp salt
$\frac{1}{4}$ tsp baking soda

1 egg, slightly beaten
1 cup low-fat buttermilk
2 Tbsp unsweetened
   applesauce
1 Tbsp canola oil
1 cup fresh blueberries (or
   use unsweetened frozen)

1. Preheat the oven to 425 degrees. Combine the dry ingredients in a mixing bowl and set aside. Combine the egg, buttermilk, applesauce, and oil and mix well.
2. Make a well in the center of the dry ingredients and pour in the liquid ingredients. Stir just until moistened. Fold in the blueberries.
3. Fill the muffin cups two-thirds full. Bake for 20–25 minutes. Remove the muffins from the pan immediately.

Starch Exchange 1	Sodium ....211 mg
Calories 75	Carbohydrate.....................14 g
Calories from Fat...............13	Dietary Fiber ....1 g
Total Fat ....1 g	Sugars...................................4 g
Saturated Fat.....................0 g	Protein..................................2 g
Cholesterol.....................12 mg	

Corn Bread Sticks

11 servings/serving size: 1 corn stick
Preparation time: 10 minutes

Corn Bread Sticks are fantastic with homemade soup. It's a great way to warm up on a chilly day!

1 cup stone-ground cornmeal
3 Tbsp flour
¼ cup unprocessed, uncooked wheat bran
1 tsp baking powder
1 Tbsp sugar

¼ tsp salt
¼ tsp baking soda
1 cup low-fat buttermilk
1 egg, slightly beaten
2 Tbsp corn oil

1. Preheat the oven to 475 degrees. Combine the dry ingredients in a large bowl and mix well. Combine the buttermilk, egg, and oil and add to the dry ingredients, stirring just until the dry ingredients are moistened.
2. Pour the batter into corn bread stick molds. If using cast-iron molds, preheat in the oven for 3 minutes before adding the batter. Bake for 12–15 minutes.

Starch Exchange 1	Cholesterol......................20 mg
Polyunsaturated Fat Exchange ....½	Sodium ....144 mg
	Carbohydrate......................15 g
Calories 101	Dietary Fiber ....2 g
Calories from Fat................33	Sugars...............................2 g
Total Fat ....4 g	Protein..............................3 g
Saturated Fat......................1 g	

Corn Bread Stuffing

12 servings/serving size: $\frac{1}{12}$ recipe
Preparation time: 10 minutes

Try this stuffing with your next roast chicken or turkey.

1 recipe Crusty Corn Bread
  (see recipe, p. 137)
1 cup celery, chopped
1 cup onion, chopped
2 slices toast, crumbled
2$\frac{1}{2}$ cups low-fat, low-sodium
  chicken broth

1$\frac{1}{2}$ tsp sage
1 tsp white pepper
$\frac{1}{2}$ tsp garlic powder
Nonstick cooking spray

1. Preheat the oven to 350 degrees. Crumble the corn bread. Cook the celery and onion in $\frac{1}{4}$ cup of the broth in a skillet until tender.
2. Add the celery mixture, remaining broth (adjust for desired degree of moistness), and remaining ingredients to the corn bread crumbs; mix well.
3. Spray a 12 x 8 x 2-inch baking dish with nonstick cooking spray. Spoon the dressing into the dish and bake for 40 minutes.

Starch Exchange	1	Cholesterol	19 mg
Fat Exchange	1	Sodium	381 mg
Calories	119	Carbohydrate	16 g
Calories from Fat	47	Dietary Fiber	2 g
Total Fat	5 g	Sugars	2 g
Saturated Fat	1 g	Protein	4 g

Crusty Corn Bread

10 servings/serving size: $\frac{1}{10}$ recipe
Preparation time: 10 minutes

A very common meal in the South is greens, pot likker (the broth, usually flavored with meat), and corn bread. You can't get much more Southern than that!

1 cup yellow cornmeal
1 Tbsp whole-wheat flour
¼ cup unprocessed,
    uncooked wheat bran
1 tsp baking soda

1 tsp salt
1 cup low-fat buttermilk
1 egg
3 Tbsp corn oil

1. Preheat the oven to 425 degrees. Combine the dry ingredients in a large bowl. Combine the buttermilk, egg, and oil and add to the dry ingredients, stirring just until the dry ingredients are moistened.
2. Pour the batter into an 8 x 8-inch pan or cast-iron skillet. (If using cast-iron, preheat the skillet in the oven for 3 minutes before adding the batter.) Bake for 20 minutes.

Starch Exchange 1	Cholesterol.....................22 mg
Polyunsaturated Fat	Sodium ....391 mg
Exchange...........................1	Carbohydrate.....................14 g
Calories 113	Dietary Fiber ....2 g
Calories from Fat.................50	Sugars................................1 g
Total Fat ....6 g	Protein................................3 g
Saturated Fat......................1 g	

Feather Rolls

20 servings/serving size: 1 roll
Preparation time: 20 minutes

Yeast breads are not as hard to make as you might think. This basic recipe can give great results. If your rolls do not turn out light and airy the first time, don't give up . . . you may have added too much flour. Try again—they're worth it!

1 pkg dry yeast
½ cup warm water
1 Tbsp sugar
½ cup skim milk
½ Tbsp canola oil
½ tsp salt
1 small egg

3½ cups bread flour (you may use part whole-wheat flour)
¼ cup unprocessed, uncooked wheat bran
¼ cup skim milk
1 tsp canola oil

1. Dissolve the yeast in warm, not hot, water. Add 1 tsp of the sugar. Heat the ½ cup of milk slightly in a saucepot; cool until just barely warm. (If the mixture is too hot, it will kill the yeast enzymes.) Add the milk to the yeast.
2. Combine the yeast mixture, remaining sugar, oil, salt, and egg in a large bowl. Combine the flour and the bran and add it to the bowl, ½ a cup at a time, until the mixture forms a dough.
3. Turn the dough out onto a floured board and knead until smooth and elastic, about 5 minutes. (You do not need to work with this dough very long because it will be made into rolls, not bread.) Place the dough in a bowl and let it rise until it doubles, about 1 hour. (The dough will rise better if it is in a warm area of the kitchen, such as on top of the stove, but not directly over any heat).

4. Punch the dough down and cut it into 4 equal pieces. With your hands, roll each quarter into a log and then cut it into 5 equal pieces. Use additional bran to keep the dough from sticking, if necessary.

5. Place the rolls on a large baking pan. Combine the ¼ cup of milk and oil and brush over the rolls. Let the rolls rise until double (about 45 minutes). Preheat the oven to 375 degrees. Bake for 20 minutes.

Starch Exchange	1½	Sodium	64 mg
Calories	103	Carbohydrate	20 g
Calories from Fat	10	Dietary Fiber	1 g
Total Fat	1 g	Sugars	1 g
Saturated Fat	0 g	Protein	4 g
Cholesterol	5 mg		

Oven-Fried Hush Puppies

10 servings/serving size: 2 Hush Puppies
Preparation time: 10 minutes

Tradition has it Hush Puppies were thrown to the hounds to keep them quiet!

1 cup stone-ground cornmeal
⅓ cup flour
¼ tsp baking soda
1 tsp baking powder
¼ tsp salt

1 Tbsp sugar
1 egg
1 cup low-fat buttermilk
3 Tbsp corn oil
1 small onion, grated

1. Preheat the oven to 425 degrees. Stir the dry ingredients together.
2. In a separate bowl, blend the buttermilk, egg, and oil. Add the grated onion, then add this mixture to the dry ingredients.
3. Stir well, then drop the batter by teaspoonfuls onto a nonstick cookie sheet. Bake for 10–12 minutes until golden brown.

Starch Exchange 1	Cholesterol......................22 mg
Polyunsaturated Fat	Sodium ....159 mg
Exchange...........................1	Carbohydrate....................17 g
Calories 131	Dietary Fiber ....1 g
Calories from Fat...............49	Sugars..................................3 g
Total Fat ....5 g	Protein..................................3 g
Saturated Fat......................1 g	

Pecan Waffles

5 servings/serving size: 1 waffle
Preparation time: 10 minutes

Try these waffles with homemade blueberry syrup: simply heat 1 cup of blueberries, 2 tsp corn syrup, and 1 Tbsp water until the blueberries pop.

1¼ cups flour
1 Tbsp sugar
2½ tsp baking powder
½ tsp salt
¼ cup unprocessed,
    uncooked wheat bran

1 egg yolk plus 2 egg whites
1½ cups skim milk
2 Tbsp canola oil
¼ cup chopped pecans

1. Sift the dry ingredients together. Beat the egg yolk, combine with the milk and oil, and stir into the dry ingredients.
2. Fold in the pecans, mixing only until blended. Beat the egg whites until stiff and fold into the batter. Cook the batter in a waffle iron.

Starch Exchange..................2½
Monounsaturated Fat
    Exchange 1½
Calories 263
    Calories from Fat................94
Total Fat ....10 g
    Saturated Fat......................1 g
Cholesterol........................44 mg
Sodium ....487 mg
Carbohydrate.......................34 g
    Dietary Fiber ....3 g
    Sugars.................................7 g
Protein................................9 g

Prune-Nut Bread

14 servings/serving size: 1 slice
Preparation time: 10 minutes

You can bake this tasty bread in three mini loaf pans and freeze some for later use.

½ cup dried prunes, chopped
2 tsp orange zest
¾ cup orange juice
2 cups whole-wheat flour
¼ cup sugar

1 Tbsp baking powder
½ tsp salt
½ tsp cinnamon
2 eggs, beaten
2 Tbsp canola oil
½ cup chopped pecans

1. Combine the prunes, orange zest, and juice in a large mixing bowl and stir gently. Let stand about 30 minutes. Add the eggs and oil to the prune mixture and stir well.
2. Preheat the oven to 350 degrees. Combine the dry ingredients in a separate bowl and mix well. Add the dry ingredients to the prune mixture and stir until blended. Fold in the pecans.
3. Pour the batter into a nonstick 9 x 5-inch loaf pan and bake for 55–60 minutes, or until a wooden toothpick inserted in the center comes out clean. Cool in the pan for 10 minutes, then remove from the pan and let cool on a wire rack.

Starch Exchange..................1½
Monounsaturated Fat
    Exchange..........................½
Calories 141
    Calories from Fat..............48
Total Fat..............................5 g
    Saturated Fat....................1 g

Cholesterol......................30 mg
Sodium ....171 mg
Carbohydrate....................21 g
    Dietary Fiber....................3 g
    Sugars..............................7 g
Protein...............................4 g

Spoon Bread

8 servings/serving size: ⅛th recipe
Preparation time: 10 minutes

This is a very, very old Southern recipe. It's served as a casserole dish.

1½ cups boiling water
1 cup cornmeal
¼ cup unprocessed,
   uncooked wheat bran
1 tsp salt

1 Tbsp butter
1 cup low-fat milk
1 large egg, lightly beaten
2 tsp baking powder

1. Preheat the oven to 375 degrees. Pour the water over the cornmeal and bran gradually, stirring until smooth. Add the salt and butter, stirring until blended. Cool 10 minutes.
2. Gradually stir in the milk and egg. Add the baking powder, stirring until blended. Pour the mixture into a 1½-quart nonstick baking dish. Bake for 40 minutes or until lightly browned.

Starch Exchange 1	Cholesterol ....31 mg
Saturated Fat Exchange........½	Sodium ....421 mg
Calories 101	Carbohydrate....................17 g
Calories from Fat...............23	Dietary Fiber ....2 g
Total Fat ....3 g	Sugars................................1 g
Saturated Fat......................1 g	Protein................................4 g

Sweet Potato Rolls

20 servings/serving size: 1 roll
Preparation time: 20 minutes

You can substitute squash or pumpkin for the sweet potato in this recipe.

1 pkg dry yeast
¼ cup warm water
2 Tbsp canola oil
½ cup skim milk, scalded
2 Tbsp sugar
1 tsp salt
½ tsp nutmeg
½ tsp cinnamon
¾ cup cooked, mashed sweet
   potatoes

1 egg, beaten
3 cups bread flour (you may
   use part whole-wheat flour)
⅓ cup unprocessed,
   uncooked wheat bran
Nonstick cooking spray
2 Tbsp canola oil

1. Dissolve the yeast in warm water and let stand for 5 minutes. Combine the oil, milk, sugar, salt, and spices in a large mixing bowl. Cool until lukewarm.
2. Add the sweet potatoes, egg, and yeast mixture, mixing well. Gradually stir in enough flour and bran to make a soft dough.
3. Turn the dough out onto a floured surface and knead until smooth and elastic, about 8 minutes. Spray a bowl with nonstick cooking spray and place the dough in the bowl, turning to grease top.
4. Cover the dough and let it rise in a warm place for 1 hour or until doubled. Punch the dough down and cut into 4 equal pieces. Let the dough rest for 5–10 minutes.

5. Preheat the oven to 375 degrees. Cut each piece of dough into 5 rolls. Roll each piece into a ball.

6. Place the balls of dough on a large, nonstick cookie sheet, allowing 1½ inches between each roll. Brush the roll tops with oil. Bake for 20–25 minutes or until browned.

Starch Exchange..................1½	Cholesterol......................11 mg
Monounsaturated Fat	Sodium ....124 mg
Exchange ....½	Carbohydrate......................20 g
Calories 127	Dietary Fiber ....1 g
Calories from Fat................32	Sugars...................................3 g
Total Fat................................4 g	Protein..................................4 g
Saturated Fat......................0 g	

Whole-Wheat Soft Pretzels

30 servings/serving size: 1 pretzel
Preparation time: 25 minutes

These chewy pretzels make a great afternoon snack!

¼ cup warm water
1 pkg dry yeast
1⅓ cups warm water
1 Tbsp brown sugar
1 tsp salt

5 cups whole-wheat flour
¼ cup gluten flour
½ cup unprocessed,
    uncooked wheat bran
Baking soda

1. In a large bowl, mix the ¼ cup warm water and the yeast until the yeast dissolves. Stir in the additional 1⅓ cups warm water, brown sugar, and salt. Slowly add the flours to the mixture, stirring constantly.
2. As the dough stiffens, knead the remaining flour into the dough. Knead the dough until it is stretchy and smooth. Let the dough rise for 30–40 minutes in a warm location.
3. Heat the oven to 475 degrees. Sprinkle 2 nonstick cookie sheets with bran. Divide the dough into 3 equal pieces. Divide each equal piece in half.
4. Divide each half into 5 equal pieces. Roll each piece out to make a rope. Tie the rope into a pretzel shape. Let the pretzel rest for 10 minutes.
5. Fill a frying pan with water. For each cup of water in the pan, add 1 Tbsp of baking soda. Heat the water until hot, but not boiling.

6. Lower the pretzels, 2 at a time, into the water for 30 seconds. Remove the pretzels and place on the cookie sheets.
7. Sprinkle the pretzels with bran and bake for 8 minutes or until golden brown.

Starch Exchange ....1 Sodium ....79 mg
Calories ....76 Carbohydrate......................17 g
   Calories from Fat 4   Dietary Fiber ....3 g
Total Fat ....0 g   Sugars.................................1 g
   Saturated Fat ....0 g Protein.................................3 g
Cholesterol ....0 g

Desserts

Amaretto Chocolate Mousse
Apple Crisp
Applesauce Raisin Bars
Baked Egg Custard
Banana Meringue Pudding
Benne (Sesame) Seed Cookies
Bread Pudding
Butternut Squash Pie
Carolina Rice Pudding
Custard-Style Vanilla Ice Cream
Date-Nut Sour Cream Pound Cake
Fresh Fruit Tarts
Healthy Pie Crust
Individual Strawberry Tarts
Marshmallow-Chocolate Sauce
Mississippi Mud Cake
Peach Cobbler
Pecan Meringue Cookies
Pineapple Upside-Down Cake
Raspberry Fudge Brownies
Roughed-Up Chocolate Chip Cookies
Strawberry Shortcake
Sweet Potato Pie
Vanilla Pudding
Whole-Wheat Walnut Cookies

Amaretto Chocolate Mousse

8 servings/serving size: $\frac{1}{2}$ cup
Preparation time: 25 minutes

This is a great dessert to serve at a holiday party.

1 envelope unflavored
  gelatin
1$\frac{1}{2}$ cups low-fat milk
2 egg yolks
$\frac{1}{2}$ cup sugar

$\frac{1}{3}$ cup cocoa
2 Tbsp amaretto
4 egg whites, room
  temperature
12 strawberry halves

1. Combine the gelatin and $\frac{1}{2}$ cup milk in a medium saucepot. Stir well and let stand 1 minute. Cook over medium heat, stirring constantly, for 1 minute or until the gelatin dissolves.
2. In a small bowl, beat together the remaining 1 cup milk and the egg yolks. Add the yolk mixture, $\frac{1}{4}$ cup sugar, and the cocoa to saucepot and stir well.
3. Cook over medium heat, stirring constantly, for 8 minutes or until the mixture is smooth and thickened. Remove the mousse from heat; stir in the amaretto and chill for 20 minutes.
4. Beat the egg whites in a medium bowl until foamy. Gradually add the remaining sugar, 1 Tbsp at a time, beating until stiff peaks form.
5. Slowly add the chilled chocolate mixture to the beaten egg whites, folding gently. Spoon the mixture into 8 individual dessert dishes.

6. Chill at least 2 hours. Garnish with strawberry halves before serving.

Carbohydrate Exchange 1½

Calories 119

   Calories from Fat 24

Total Fat ....3 g

   Saturated Fat ....1 g

Cholesterol ....57 mg

Sodium ....54 mg

Carbohydrate ....19 mg

   Dietary Fiber ....1 g

   Sugars...............................17 g

Protein...................................5 g

Apple Crisp

4 servings/serving size: ½ cup
Preparation time: 15 minutes

Granny Smith apples work very well in this dish.

4 cups peeled, sliced apples
¼ cup water
4 tsp brown sugar
2 tsp lemon juice
¾ tsp cinnamon

½ cup quick-cooking oats or
    old-fashioned rolled oats
2 Tbsp chopped walnuts
1 Tbsp canola oil

1. Preheat the oven to 375 degrees. Combine the apples, water, sugar, lemon juice, and cinnamon in a medium bowl. Toss to coat the apples. Spread the slices out in an ungreased 6-inch-square baking dish.
2. In a small bowl, combine the remaining ingredients and mix well. Sprinkle the topping over the apples. Bake for 50 minutes or until the apples are tender and the topping is browned. Serve warm or chilled.

Starch Exchange 1	Cholesterol ....0 mg
Fruit Exchange.......................1	Sodium ....3 mg
Fat Exchange 1	Carbohydrate.....................28 g
Calories 169	Dietary Fiber ....3 g
Calories from Fat 57	Sugars...............................19 g
Total Fat ....6 g	Protein................................2 g
Saturated Fat ....1 g	

Applesauce Raisin Bars

24 servings/serving size: 1 bar
Preparation time: 15 minutes

These bars freeze well, so keep a supply on hand for unexpected visitors!

1 cup water
1 cup raisins
1 cup unsweetened
   applesauce
2 eggs
1/3 cup pure maple syrup
1/2 cup canola oil

1 tsp vanilla
1 tsp baking soda
2 cups flour, part or all
   whole-wheat
1 1/4 tsp cinnamon
1/2 tsp nutmeg

1. Preheat the oven to 350 degrees. Cook the raisins in water until they are soft. Drain off water. In a medium bowl, combine the raisins, applesauce, eggs, syrup, oil, and vanilla.
2. Combine the remaining ingredients and add to the medium bowl. Mix well. Bake in a nonstick 9 x 12-inch pan for 30 minutes. Cool 10–15 minutes before serving.

Starch Exchange 1
Monounsaturated Fat
   Exchange............................1
Calories 118
   Calories from Fat................48
Total Fat..................................5 g
   Saturated Fat.......................0 g

Cholesterol......................18 mg
Sodium ....59 mg
Carbohydrate.....................17 g
   Dietary Fiber ....1 g
   Sugars..................................8 g
Protein...................................2 g

Baked Egg Custard

4 servings/serving size: 1 custard cup
Preparation time: 10 minutes

You can also add fresh or frozen blueberries or peaches to this custard after it's been in the oven about 20 minutes.

3 eggs
⅛ tsp cinnamon
⅛ tsp nutmeg
¼ tsp salt
3 Tbsp pure maple syrup

1 tsp vanilla
2 cups low-fat milk
Nonstick cooking spray
Dash nutmeg

1. Preheat the oven to 350 degrees. Beat the eggs, slowly adding the next 6 ingredients. Spray 4 custard cups with nonstick cooking spray. Pour the custard into the cups and sprinkle nutmeg on top.
2. Place the cups in a roasting pan. Carefully fill the pan with hot water, almost to the level of the custard. Bake for 40–50 minutes.
3. When you remove the pan from the oven, remove the cups from the pan; otherwise the custard will continue to cook. Cool to room temperature, then chill before serving.

Carbohydrate Exchange.........1	Cholesterol....................169 mg
Medium-Fat Meat	Sodium ....255 mg
Exchange...........................1	Carbohydrate.....................16 g
Calories 156	Dietary Fiber ....0 g
Calories from Fat................55	Sugars................................16 g
Total Fat ....6 g	Protein...................................9 g
Saturated Fat......................3 g	

Banana Meringue Pudding

4 servings/serving size: ½ cup
Preparation time: 30 minutes

This special dessert is time-consuming to prepare, but everyone will love its old-fashioned flavor!

1 recipe Vanilla Pudding (see recipe, p. 177)
2 medium-ripe bananas
12 vanilla wafers
2 egg whites, room temperature
¼ tsp cream of tartar
1 Tbsp sugar

1. Prepare the Vanilla Pudding (do not chill). Preheat the oven to 400 degrees. Line 4 individual oven-proof custard dishes with 3 vanilla wafers. Slice ½ banana into each dish. Pour ¼ of the pudding on top.
2. Beat the egg whites, cream of tartar, and sugar until soft peaks form. Spread the meringue over the individual puddings. Bake for 8–10 minutes or until browned.

Carbohydrate Exchange	3	Cholesterol	115 mg
Fat Exchange	½	Sodium	203 mg
Calories	248	Carbohydrate	44 g
Calories from Fat	43	Dietary Fiber	2 g
Total Fat	5 g	Sugars	29 g
Saturated Fat	1 g	Protein	8 g

Benne (Sesame) Seed Cookies

18 servings/serving size: 4 cookies
Preparation time: 15 minutes

Benne seed cookies (wafers) are found in many specialty stores in the South. This version cuts the fat and sugar in half, so enjoy!

½ cup butter
½ cup brown sugar
2 eggs plus 1 egg white
¼ tsp baking powder
1 cup whole-wheat flour
Dash salt

⅔ cup toasted benne (sesame) seeds
⅓ cup unprocessed, uncooked wheat bran
1 tsp vanilla

1. Preheat the oven to 350 degrees. Cream the butter and sugar, then add the other ingredients in order. Cut wax paper to fit on a cookie sheet.
2. Drop the dough from the tip of a teaspoon, allowing at least an inch all around for spreading. Bake until brown around edges or brown all over (depending on your preference), about 8–10 minutes.
3. When done, lift the entire paper, including the cookies, off the baking sheet onto a flat surface. Remove the cookies when completely cool.

Carbohydrate Exchange.........1	Cholesterol......................38 mg
Fat Exchange 1½	Sodium ....70 mg
Calories 135	Carbohydrate....................13 g
Calories from Fat...............79	Dietary Fiber ....2 g
Total Fat ....9 g	Sugars................................7 g
Saturated Fat.....................4 g	Protein................................3 g

Bread Pudding

10 servings/serving size: 1 slice
Preparation time: 15 minutes

Try this classic pudding at your next brunch.

6 slices whole-wheat, day-old bread	**1 Tbsp canola oil**
⅓ cup raisins	**2 eggs**
1 tsp cinnamon	**¼ cup sugar**
1 tsp nutmeg	**2 cups low-fat milk**

1. Preheat the oven to 350 degrees. Break the bread into small pieces and place in a nonstick 8 x 8-inch baking pan. Mix in the raisins, cinnamon, nutmeg, and canola oil.
2. In a medium bowl, mix the eggs, sugar, and milk. Pour the milk mixture over the bread pieces in the pan. Set aside for 5 minutes or until the bread soaks up the milk.
3. Cover the pan with foil and bake for 30 minutes. Remove the foil and continue baking for another 30 minutes. Let the pudding cool for 30 minutes before serving.

Carbohydrate Exchange.....1½	Cholesterol.....................46 mg
Fat Exchange ....½	Sodium ....127 mg
Calories 127	Carbohydrate.....................19 g
Calories from Fat...............37	Dietary Fiber ....1 g
Total Fat...............................4 g	Sugars...............................11 g
Saturated Fat.....................1 g	Protein.................................5 g

Butternut Squash Pie

8 servings/serving size: 1 slice
Preparation time: 20 minutes

1 2-lb butternut squash	¹⁄₄ tsp salt
¹⁄₃ cup pure maple syrup	1 12-oz can evaporated skim
1 tsp cinnamon	milk
¹⁄₂ tsp allspice	2 eggs, beaten
¹⁄₂ tsp nutmeg	1 Healthy Pie Crust, unbaked
¹⁄₄ tsp cloves	(see recipe, p. 163)

1. Preheat the oven to 350 degrees. Slice the squash in half lengthwise and remove the seeds. Place the squash cut side down in a shallow baking pan and add water to a depth of ³⁄₄ inch.
2. Bake, uncovered, for 45 minutes or until the squash is tender. Drain and cool. Peel the squash and mash the pulp thoroughly. Measure out 2 cups of mashed squash.
3. Raise the oven temperature to 400 degrees. Combine the squash, syrup, spices, and salt; mix well. Gradually stir in the milk and eggs.
4. Pour the mixture into the pie shell and bake for 10 minutes. Reduce the heat to 350 degrees and bake an additional 40 minutes or until set. Cool before serving.

Carbohydrate Exchange.........2	Cholesterol......................55 mg
Monounsaturated Fat	Sodium ....293 mg
Exchange............................2	Carbohydrate......................31 g
Calories 246	Dietary Fiber ....4 g
Calories from Fat..............101	Sugars................................15 g
Total Fat ....11 g	Protein................................8 g
Saturated Fat......................1 g	

Carolina Rice Pudding

6 servings/serving size: ½ cup
Preparation time: 15 minutes

You can also bake this pudding in individual custard cups.

2 eggs plus 2 egg whites
3 Tbsp pure maple syrup
2 cups skim milk
1 Tbsp corn oil

¾ cup cooked brown rice
Dash salt
½ tsp cinnamon

1. Preheat the oven to 350 degrees. Separate the 2 eggs. Mix the egg yolks and the maple syrup. Add the milk slowly. Beat the 4 egg whites until stiff and mix with the yolk mixture.
2. Stir the oil into the rice. Pour the rice into a 1½-quart baking dish and add half of the egg mixture. Stir well. Pour the rest of the egg mixture over it and top with cinnamon. Bake until set, about 25–35 minutes.

Carbohydrate Exchange	1	Cholesterol	72 mg
Fat Exchange	1	Sodium	107 mg
Calories	135	Carbohydrate	17 g
Calories from Fat	41	Dietary Fiber	0 g
Total Fat	5 g	Sugars	10 g
Saturated Fat	1 g	Protein	7 g

Custard-Style Vanilla Ice Cream

8 servings/serving size: $^1/_3$ cup
Preparation time: 15 minutes

Try serving this creamy dessert with fresh raspberries or strawberries.

2 cups 1% milk	$^1/_2$ cup sugar
2 tsp vanilla	$^1/_8$ tsp salt
3 egg yolks	1 cup light cream

1. Chill the container of an ice-cream maker or a 9 x 13-inch baking pan in the freezer. Warm the milk in a small saucepot over low heat until bubbles appear around the edges. Remove from heat and add the vanilla.
2. In a medium bowl, whisk the egg yolk until thick and fluffy. Gradually beat in the sugar and salt. Pour the cooled milk through a strainer over the eggs and beat with a wire whisk until well combined. Stir in the cream and set aside.
3. Pour the mixture into the ice-cream maker and process according to manufacturer's directions, or pour into the chilled baking pan and freeze until firm.

Carbohydrate Exchange	1	Cholesterol	104 mg
Saturated Fat Exchange	$1^1/_2$	Sodium	80 mg
Calories	160	Carbohydrate	17 g
Calories from Fat	80	Dietary Fiber	0 g
Total Fat	9 g	Sugars	17 g
Saturated Fat	5 g	Protein	4 g

Date-Nut Sour Cream Pound Cake

24 servings/serving size: 1 slice
Preparation time: 15 minutes

Your guests will love this low-fat, delicious pound cake.

4 Tbsp butter	**¼ tsp baking powder**
1 cup sugar	**8 oz lite sour cream**
3 eggs, separated	**¼ tsp mace**
2 cups whole-wheat flour	**1 tsp lemon juice**
¼ tsp salt	**¼ cup chopped dates**
¼ tsp baking soda	**¼ cup chopped pecans**

1. Preheat the oven to 300 degrees. Allow all ingredients to come to room temperature. Cream the butter and the sugar. Add the egg yolks and mix well.
2. Sift the flour, salt, baking soda, and baking powder together. Add the flour mixture and the sour cream alternately to the butter mixture. Add the mace, lemon juice, dates, and pecans.
3. Beat the egg whites until stiff and fold into the mixture. Bake in a nonstick tube pan for 90 minutes or until a toothpick comes out clean.

Carbohydrate Exchange	1	Cholesterol	35 mg
Fat Exchange	½	Sodium	75 mg
Calories	114	Carbohydrate	18 g
Calories from Fat	38	Dietary Fiber	1 g
Total Fat	4 g	Sugars	10 g
Saturated Fat	2 g	Protein	3 g

Fresh Fruit Tarts

4 servings/serving size: 1 tart
Preparation time: 15 minutes

These are great tarts to make in the summer, when strawberries and peaches are fresh. Try to prepare this recipe within 4 hours of serving to keep the nut crust from getting soggy.

4 oz fresh almonds or
   toasted hazelnuts
¼ cup raisins
2 Tbsp pure maple syrup
1 small banana, thickly sliced

1 cup sliced strawberries or
   whole blueberries
2 small peaches, sliced
1 Tbsp lemon juice
1 small kiwi fruit

1. Using a blender or food processor, chop the nuts and raisins until finely chopped. Add the maple syrup and stir gently to mix. Divide the mixture into 4 tart or custard dishes and press out into a crust.
2. Divide the fruit among the tart dishes and drizzle with lemon juice. Top each tart with 2 slices of kiwi. Chill 1–2 hours before serving.

Carbohydrate Exchange.....2½
Monounsaturated Fat
   Exchange............................3
Calories 292
   Calories from Fat..............134
Total Fat ....15 g
   Saturated Fat......................1 g

Cholesterol..........................0 mg
Sodium ....9 mg
Carbohydrate ....39 mg
   Dietary Fiber ....7 g
   Sugars..............................26 g
Protein...................................6 g

Healthy Pie Crust

8 servings/serving size: ⅛ crust
Preparation time: 10 minutes

This pie crust has a slightly chewier texture than traditional crusts. It's great with fruit pies.

¾ cup whole-wheat flour
¼ cup unprocessed,
   uncooked wheat bran
¼ cup old-fashioned oats,
   uncooked

½ tsp salt
⅓ cup canola oil
6 Tbsp ice water

Preheat the oven to 375 degrees. Mix the dry ingredients. Stir the oil into the dry ingredients, then mix in the water with a fork. Press into a 9-inch pie pan. Bake for 15 minutes.

Starch Exchange....................½	Cholesterol.........................0 mg
Monounsaturated Fat	Sodium ....146 mg
Exchange...........................2	Carbohydrate......................11 g
Calories 135	Dietary Fiber ....3 g
Calories from Fat 89	Sugars..................................0 g
Total Fat ....10 g	Protein..................................2 g
Saturated Fat ....1 g	

Individual Strawberry Tarts

6 servings/serving size: 1 tart
Preparation time: 15 minutes

Fresh strawberries are delicious in these tarts.

Pastry for one 9-inch shell
1 4-oz pkg artificially
  sweetened strawberry
  gelatin

4 cups whole strawberries,
  caps off
1 Tbsp lemon juice

1. Preheat the oven to 450 degrees. Roll out the pastry and cut it into six circles to fit individual tart pans. Prick the bottoms and sides of the pastry circles. Bake the pastry 10–12 minutes until browned.
2. Soften the gelatin in some of the cold water called for in the package directions. Mash 2 cups of the berries. Cook the berries, lemon juice, and remaining water until the mixture boils.
3. Remove from heat and add the softened gelatin, stirring to dissolve. Chill until the mixture begins to thicken. Arrange the strawberries in the tart shells and pour the gelatin mixture over the top. Chill before serving.

Carbohydrate Exchange..........1	Cholesterol.........................0 mg
Monounsaturated Fat	Sodium ....175 mg
Exchange......................1½	Carbohydrate.....................18 g
Calories 144	Dietary Fiber ....3 g
Calories from Fat................66	Sugars..................................5 g
Total Fat ....7 g	Protein..................................2 g
Saturated Fat......................2 g	

Marshmallow-Chocolate Sauce

24 servings/serving size: 1 Tbsp
Preparation time: 15 minutes

Try this topping over ice milk, angel food cake, or fresh fruit.

⅓ cup mini marshmallows
1 Tbsp plus 2 tsp
　unsweetened cocoa
1 Tbsp cornstarch
1 cup skim milk

1 Tbsp light corn syrup
1 tsp vanilla
¼ tsp cinnamon
¼ cup mini marshmallows
1 Tbsp chopped pecans

1. Combine the ⅓ cup marshmallows, cocoa, and cornstarch in a small saucepot. Gradually stir in the milk and corn syrup. Cook over medium heat, stirring constantly, until thickened.
2. Remove the sauce from the heat and stir in the vanilla and cinnamon. Let cool. Stir in ¼ cup marshmallows and the pecans before serving.

Free Food
Calories 13
　Calories from Fat 2
Total Fat ....0 g
　Saturated Fat ....0 g
Cholesterol ....0 mg

Sodium ....7 mg
Carbohydrate........................3 g
　Dietary Fiber ....0 g
　Sugars..................................2 g
Protein..................................0 g

Mississippi Mud Cake

12 servings/serving size: 1 slice
Preparation time: 20 minutes

Baking this rich, chocolaty cake on foil makes it easier to remove it from the pan. You'll love the crunchy pecans and chewy marshmallows on top!

4 Tbsp butter
$\frac{1}{2}$ cup brown sugar
$\frac{1}{3}$ cup sugar
1 oz unsweetened chocolate, melted
$1\frac{1}{2}$ Tbsp whipping cream
1 tsp vanilla
2 large eggs, room temperature
1 4-oz jar baby prunes, pureed

$\frac{3}{4}$ cup whole-wheat pastry flour
$\frac{1}{4}$ cup unsweetened Dutch-processed cocoa, sifted
$\frac{1}{4}$ cup unprocessed, uncooked wheat bran
$\frac{1}{4}$ tsp baking soda
Dash salt
$\frac{1}{2}$ cup mini marshmallows
$\frac{1}{2}$ cup chopped, toasted pecans

1. Preheat the oven to 350 degrees. Line a 9 x 9-inch cake pan with aluminum foil, allowing the foil to drape over the edges. Spray the foil with nonstick cooking spray.
2. Cream the butter and sugars in a medium bowl until fluffy. Beat in the chocolate, whipping cream, and vanilla.
3. Add the eggs, one at a time, beating well after each addition. Stir in the prunes. Sift the flour, cocoa, bran, baking soda, and salt together and stir into the batter.
4. Bake about 20 minutes until a toothpick inserted into center comes out clean.

5. Before removing the cake from the pan, sprinkle the marshmallows and pecans on top. Return to the oven and bake just until the marshmallows begin to melt, about 5 minutes. Cool the cake in the pan on a rack. Using the foil as an aid, lift the cake from the pan. Remove the foil and serve.

Carbohydrate Exchange	2	Cholesterol	49 mg
Fat Exchange	1	Sodium	85 mg
Calories	196	Carbohydrate	27 g
Calories from Fat	90	Dietary Fiber	3 g
Total Fat	10 g	Sugars	18 g
Saturated Fat	4 g	Protein	3 g

Peach Cobbler

8 servings/serving size: ⅛ recipe
Preparation time: 15 minutes

**8 large, ripe peaches, peeled
  and sliced**
2 Tbsp lemon juice
⅓ cup sugar
¾ cup whole-wheat flour
**⅓ cup unprocessed,
  uncooked wheat bran**

1 tsp cinnamon
1 tsp ginger
Nonstick cooking spray
Pastry for 9-inch pie

1. Preheat the oven to 425 degrees. Combine the peaches and lemon juice and toss to mix. Combine the remaining ingredients and add to the peaches, mixing lightly. Spray a 9-inch-square baking dish with nonstick cooking spray. Spoon the peach mixture evenly into the dish.
2. Roll out the pastry to a ⅛-inch thickness; cut into ½-inch strips. Lay half the strips across the filling, spacing them about ¾ inch apart. Repeat with the remaining strips, arranging them in the opposite direction to form a latticework. Bake for 10 minutes; reduce heat to 350 degrees and bake for an additional 40 minutes.

Carbohydrate Exchange.........3	Cholesterol.........................0 mg
Monounsaturated Fat	Sodium.................................147
Exchange............................1	Carbohydrate......................48 g
Calories 282	Dietary Fiber ....8 g
Calories from Fat................93	Sugars.................................23 g
Total Fat..............................10 g	Protein.................................5 g
Saturated Fat......................1 g	

Pecan Meringue Cookies

12 servings/serving size: 2 cookies
Preparation time: 15 minutes

These cookies are elegant served with afternoon tea.

3 egg whites
⅛ tsp salt
¾ cup brown sugar
3 Tbsp canola oil
1 tsp vanilla

2 Tbsp flour
½ cup finely chopped
   pecans
Nonstick cooking spray

1. Preheat the oven to 350 degrees. Beat the egg whites with the salt until stiff. Combine the sugar, oil, vanilla, and flour in a bowl. Fold the mixture gently into the egg whites, then fold in the nuts.
2. Cover cookie sheets with aluminum foil and spray with nonstick cooking spray. Drop the dough by slightly rounded teaspoonfuls, 3 inches apart, onto the cookie sheets. Bake for 12–15 minutes or until browned.
3. Cool on foil. If not crisp when cooled, return to the oven 2–3 minutes. Store in an airtight container.

Carbohydrate Exchange.........1
Monounsaturated Fat
   Exchange............................1
Calories 122
   Calories from Fat................58
Total Fat..................................6 g
   Saturated Fat......................0 g

Cholesterol.........................0 mg
Sodium ....42 mg
Carbohydrate.....................16 g
   Dietary Fiber.....................0 g
   Sugars.................................14 g
Protein....................................1 g

Pineapple Upside-Down Cake

8 servings/serving size: 1 slice
Preparation time: 20 minutes

This cake is the perfect ending to a summer luncheon.

1 8-oz can sliced pineapple,
   packed in its own juice
3$\frac{1}{2}$ Tbsp canola oil
1$\frac{1}{2}$ Tbsp brown sugar
6 Tbsp sugar
$\frac{1}{4}$ cup pecan halves
2 large eggs, separated, at
   room temperature

1 tsp vanilla
$\frac{3}{4}$ cup whole-wheat pastry
   flour
$\frac{3}{4}$ tsp baking powder
$\frac{1}{4}$ tsp salt

1. Preheat the oven to 325 degrees. Drain the pineapple, reserving $\frac{1}{2}$ cup of the juice. Pat the pineapple slices dry with a paper towel. In an 8-inch nonstick cake pan, combine 1$\frac{1}{2}$ Tbsp of the oil, the brown sugar, and 2 Tbsp of the white sugar. Spread the mixture evenly in the bottom of the pan.
2. Place the pineapple slices on top of the sugar mixture. Arrange the pecan halves decoratively in the center of each pineapple ring and around its edges. In a separate bowl, combine the reserved pineapple juice, the remaining 2 Tbsp oil, 2 Tbsp white sugar, the egg yolks, and the vanilla. Mix until just blended.
3. Sift together the flour, baking powder, and salt and add to the juice mixture. Mix the batter until smooth. Beat the egg whites and 2 Tbsp white sugar together until stiff

peaks form. Gently fold into the batter. Spoon the batter over the pineapple and pecans. Bake for 18–20 minutes, or until a wooden toothpick comes out clean.

4. Place a wire rack over the cake pan, invert the cake, and cool in the pan 2–3 minutes. Remove the cake from the pan and allow to cool completely. With a spatula, gently lift the cake onto a serving platter.

Carbohydrate Exchange	1½	Cholesterol	53 mg
Fat Exchange	1½	Sodium	124 mg
Calories	193	Carbohydrate	25 g
Calories from Fat	85	Dietary Fiber	1 g
Total Fat	9 g	Sugars	16 g
Saturated Fat	1 g	Protein	3 g

Raspberry Fudge Brownies

16 servings/serving size: 1 brownie
Preparation time: 20 minutes

¼ cup plus 2 Tbsp butter
¼ cup plus 2 Tbsp
  unsweetened cocoa
½ cup sugar
2 large eggs, beaten
½ tsp vanilla

3 Tbsp warm water
½ cup whole-wheat flour
⅛ tsp salt
1 10-oz pkg frozen
  raspberries
Nonstick cooking spray

1. Preheat the oven to 350 degrees. Combine the butter and cocoa in a large saucepot. Cook over low heat, stirring constantly, until the butter melts and the mixture becomes smooth. Remove from heat and let cool slightly.
2. Add the sugar, eggs, and vanilla to the cocoa mixture, stirring well to combine. Stir in the water. Combine the flour and salt and add to the cocoa mixture, stirring well to combine. Gently fold the raspberries into the cocoa mixture.
3. Spoon the batter into an 8-inch-square nonstick baking pan. Bake for 20 minutes or until a wooden toothpick inserted in the center comes out clean. Let the brownies cool completely, then cut into 2-inch squares.

Carbohydrate Exchange	½	Cholesterol	19 mg
Saturated Fat Exchange	½	Sodium	36 mg
Calories	51	Carbohydrate	6 g
Calories from Fat	25	Dietary Fiber	1 g
Total Fat	3 g	Sugars	5 g
Saturated Fat	2 g	Protein	1 g

Roughed-Up Chocolate Chip Cookies

48 servings/serving size: 1 cookie
Preparation time: 15 minutes

This recipe produces a very crisp cookie.

2¼ cups whole-wheat flour
¾ cup unprocessed,
  uncooked wheat bran
1 tsp baking soda
⅓ cup butter
¼ cup sugar

¼ cup brown sugar
2 eggs
½ cup chopped walnuts
1 cup semisweet chocolate
  morsels

1. Preheat the oven to 375 degrees. In a small bowl, combine the flour, bran, and baking soda. In a large bowl, cream the butter and sugar. Beat in the eggs.
2. Gradually add the flour mixture to the large bowl, mixing well. Stir in the nuts and chocolate. Drop by rounded teaspoonfuls onto ungreased cookie sheets. Bake for 8–10 minutes.

Carbohydrate Exchange ....½	Cholesterol......................13 mg
Fat Exchange ....½	Sodium ....44 mg
Calories 69	Carbohydrate........................9 g
Calories from Fat................32	Dietary Fiber ....1 g
Total Fat ....4 g	Sugars....................................4 g
Saturated Fat.....................2 g	Protein..................................1 g

Strawberry Shortcake

8 servings/serving size: ⅛ recipe
Preparation time: 20 minutes

Enjoy fresh strawberries in this recipe—they only come around once a year!

1¾ cups whole-wheat pastry flour	1 quart fresh strawberries, sliced
2 Tbsp sugar	1 Tbsp sugar
1 tsp baking soda	½ cup whipping cream
3 Tbsp butter	2 Tbsp powdered sugar
¾ cup low-fat buttermilk	

1. Preheat the oven to 475 degrees. In a large bowl, sift together the flour, sugar, and baking soda. Using a pastry blender or 2 knives, cut the butter into the flour mixture until coarse crumbs form. With a fork, quickly stir in the buttermilk until a soft dough forms.
2. On a lightly floured surface, gently roll out the dough to a ½-inch thickness. Using a 2½-inch biscuit cutter, cut out the biscuits. Gather trimmings, re-roll, and cut out more biscuits. You should have 8 biscuits. Place them on a nonstick cookie sheet.
3. Place the biscuits on the middle rack in the oven and reduce the oven temperature to 425 degrees. Bake until golden, about 12–15 minutes. Place the biscuits on a wire rack and cool slightly.
4. Combine the strawberries and sugar in a medium bowl and mix well. Puree about ¼ of the mixture in a blender or food processor. Add the puree back to the berries. Whip the cream with the powdered sugar.

5. Split the biscuits in half horizontally. Place the bottom halves on serving plates. Top each with some strawberry filling and cover with the biscuit tops. Pile some more filling on top and garnish with 2 Tbsp whipping cream.

Carbohydrate Exchange	2	Cholesterol	34 mg
Saturated Fat Exchange	2	Sodium	236 mg
Calories	238	Carbohydrate	32 g
Calories from Fat	100	Dietary Fiber	5 g
Total Fat	11 g	Sugars	12 g
Saturated Fat	7 g	Protein	5 g

Sweet Potato Pie

8 servings/serving size: 1 slice
Preparation time: 15 minutes

Try serving this pie instead of pumpkin pie for a great holiday dessert!

2½ cups sweet potatoes, drained and mashed
¼ cup pure maple syrup
1 cup skim milk
3 eggs
1 Tbsp butter, melted
1 tsp vanilla

½ tsp cinnamon
¼ tsp nutmeg
½ tsp allspice
¼ tsp salt
1 Healthy Pie Crust, unbaked (see recipe, p. 163)

1. Preheat the oven to 375 degrees. Combine the sweet potatoes, syrup, and milk in a large bowl and beat with an electric mixer at low speed until smooth. Add the eggs, one at a time, beating well after each addition.
2. Add the remaining ingredients, beating just until blended. Pour the mixture into the pastry shell. Bake for 50–55 minutes or until set. Cool before serving.

Carbohydrate Exchange.........2
Monounsaturated Fat
   Exchange 2½
Calories 271
   Calories from Fat...............121
Total Fat ....13 g
   Saturated Fat......................2 g

Cholesterol......................84 mg
Sodium ....308 mg
Carbohydrate......................33 g
   Dietary Fiber......................4 g
   Sugars................................18 g
Protein.................................7 g

Vanilla Pudding

4 servings/serving size: ½ cup
Preparation time: 20 minutes

2 eggs
2 cups skim milk, divided
2 Tbsp cornstarch

¼ cup sugar
⅛ tsp salt
1 tsp vanilla

1. In a small bowl, lightly beat the eggs and set aside. In another bowl, whisk ¾ cup milk into the cornstarch until completely smooth.
2. In a medium saucepot, combine the remaining milk, sugar, and salt. Bring to a boil over high heat, whisking constantly, then remove from heat.
3. Whisk the cornstarch mixture into the hot milk mixture. Bring to a boil over medium-high heat and boil for 2 minutes, whisking constantly.
4. Slowly whisk 1 cup of the hot mixture into the egg mixture. Pour this mixture back into the pot. Cook over medium-low heat for 2 minutes, whisking constantly. Do not boil. Remove the pudding from heat.
5. Add the vanilla and blend well. Pour the pudding into serving dishes and cool to room temperature. Cover and chill for 1 hour. Garnish with fresh berries or mint leaves.

Carbohydrate Exchange	1½	Cholesterol	108 mg
Fat Exchange	½	Sodium	165 mg
Calories	144	Carbohydrate	22 g
Calories from Fat	24	Dietary Fiber	0 g
Total Fat	3 g	Sugars	18 g
Saturated Fat	1 g	Protein	7 g

Whole-Wheat Walnut Cookies

20 servings/serving size: 2 cookies
Preparation time: 20 minutes

These spicy cookies taste great with hot tea.

½ cup butter
½ cup brown sugar
2 eggs
¼ cup orange juice
1½ tsp orange zest

2 cups whole-wheat flour
½ cup walnuts, finely
   chopped
1 tsp pumpkin pie spice

1. Cream the butter and sugar. Add the eggs, one at a time, and beat well. Mix in the orange juice and zest. Add the dry ingredients and mix well.
2. Refrigerate until firm, about 1–2 hours. Preheat the oven to 375 degrees. Roll out the dough to ¼-inch thickness and cut into various shapes. Bake the cookies on a nonstick cookie sheet for 10–12 minutes.

Carbohydrate Exchange.........1
Fat Exchange 1
Calories 133
   Calories from Fat.................67
Total Fat...................................7 g
   Saturated Fat......................3 g
Cholesterol......................34 mg
Sodium ....59 mg
Carbohydrate......................15 g
   Dietary Fiber ....2 g
   Sugars..................................6 g
Protein....................................3 g

Index

Alphabetical List of Recipes

Baked Beets, 91
Pickled Beets, 105

Benne (Sesame) Seeds
Benne (Sesame) Seed Biscuits, 133
Benne (Sesame) Seed Cocktail Wafers, 14
Benne (Sesame) Seed Cookies, 156

Berries
Blueberry Buttermilk Muffins, 134
Individual Strawberry Tarts, 164
Raspberry Fudge Brownies, 172
Strawberry Shortcake, 174

Cakes
Date-Nut Sour Cream Pound Cake, 161
Mississippi Mud Cake, 166
Pineapple Upside-Down Cake, 170
Strawberry Shortcake, 174

Cheese
Cheese Grits Souffle, 93
Cheese Grits with Turnip Greens, 94
Macaroni and Cheese Pie, 71

Chicken (see Poultry)

Chocolate
Amaretto Chocolate Mousse, 150
Marshmallow-Chocolate Sauce, 165
Raspberry Fudge Brownies, 172
Roughed-Up Chocolate Chip Cookies, 173

Cookies
Benne (Sesame) Seed Cookies, 156
Pecan Meringue Cookies, 169
Roughed-Up Chocolate Chip Cookies, 173
Whole-Wheat Walnut Cookies, 178

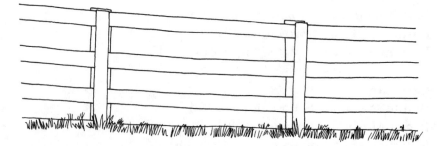

Spinach
Creamed Spinach, 97
Spinach Salad, 57
Spinach-Vegetable Dip, 25

Squash
Baked Acorn Squash, 90
Butternut Squash Pie, 158
Pumpkin Soup, 36
Squash Casserole, 112

Strawberries (see Berries)

Sweet Potatoes
Sweet Potato and Apple Salad, 58
Sweet Potato Crisps, 113
Sweet Potato Pie, 176
Sweet Potato Pone, 114
Sweet Potato Rolls, 144
Sweet Potato Souffle, 115

Tomatoes
Green Bean Salad with Sliced Tomatoes, 49
Oven-Fried Green Tomatoes, 104
Swiss Chard with Tomatoes, 116
Tomato Aspic, 59

Turkey (see Poultry)

About the Author

Marti Chitwood, RD, CDE, is a diabetes education consultant who lectures at the local, regional, national, and international levels on the topics of nutrition, wellness, and diabetes management. An educator and consultant for over fifteen years, Marti has received numerous honors, including the American Diabetes Association (ADA) Diabetes Educator of the Year. She has served on the National Board of the ADA, and was a national nominee to serve on the American Association of Diabetes Educators (AADE) Board of Directors. She remains an active member of the ADA, AADE, and the American Dietetic Association.

Marti participated in the Diabetes Control and Complications Trial (DCCT) as a research dietitian for seven years. She has been the owner and director of Marti Chitwood & Associates, a nutrition and diabetes consulting practice, for nine years. She has contributed to several professional publications, and has been featured in nationally published journals and magazines. Marti believes all people can learn to maximize their health potential through increased knowledge, skills, and motivation. Marti's new areas of interest include environmental nutrition, plant-based diets, holistic nutrition, and herbal and botanical medicine.

New Books from the American Diabetes Association Library of Cooking and Self-Care

Flavorful Seasons Cookbook

More than 400 unforgettable recipes that combine great taste with all the good-for-you benefits of a well-balanced meal. Warm up winter with recipes for Christmas, New Year's, St. Patrick's Day, and others. Welcome spring with recipes for Good Friday, Palm Sunday, Easter, Memorial Day, more. Cool off those hot summer days with fresh recipes for the Fourth of July, family barbecues, Labor Day, others. When fall chills the air you'll be ready with recipes for Halloween, Thanksgiving, and more. #CCBFS
Nonmember: $16.95; ADA Member: $13.55

Diabetic Meals In 30 Minutes—Or Less!

Put an end to bland, time-consuming meals with more than 140 fast, flavorful recipes. Complete nutrition information accompanies every recipe, and a number of "quick tips" will have you out of the kitchen and into the dining room even faster! Here's a quick sample: Salsa Salad, Oven-baked Parmesan Zucchini, Roasted Red Pepper Soup, and Layered Vanilla Parfait. #CCBDM
Nonmember: $11.95; ADA Member: $9.55

Diabetes Meal Planning Made Easy

The new Diabetes Food Pyramid helps make nutritious meal planning easier than ever. This new guide simplifies the concept by translating diabetes food guidelines into today's food choices. Simple, easy-to-follow chapters will help you understand the new food pyramid; learn all about the six food groups and how to incorporate them into a healthy diet; make smart choices when it comes to sweets, fats, and dairy products; shop smart at the grocery store; make all your meals easier by planning ahead; more. #CCBMP
Nonmember: $14.95; ADA Member: $11.95

Magic Menus for People with Diabetes

Mealtime discipline can be a major struggle—calculating exchanges, counting calories, and figuring fats is complicated and time-consuming. But now you have more than 200 low-fat, calorie-controlled selections—for breakfast, lunch, dinner, and snacks—to automatically turn the struggle into a smorgasbord. Choose from Chicken Cacciatore, Veal Piccata, Chop Suey, Beef Stroganoff, Vegetable Lasagna, plus dozens more. But don't worry about calculating all your nutrients—it's done for you automatically. #CCBMM
Nonmember: $14.95; ADA Member: $11.95

World-Class Diabetic Cooking

Travel around the world at every meal with a collection of 200 exciting new low-fat, low-calorie recipes. Features Thai, Caribbean, Scandinavian, Italian, Greek, Spanish, Chinese, Japanese, African, Mexican, Portuguese, German, and Middle Eastern recipes. All major food categories—appetizers, soups, salads, pastas, meats, breads, and desserts—are highlighted. Includes a nutrient analysis and exchanges (conveniently converted to U.S. exchanges) for each recipe. #CCBWCC

Nonmember: $12.95; ADA Member: $10.35

How to Cook for People with Diabetes

Finally, here's a collection of reader favorites from the delicious, nutritious recipes featured every month in *Diabetes Forecast.* But you don't only get ideas for pizza, chicken, unique holiday foods, vegetarian recipes and more, you also get nutrient analysis and exchanges for each recipe. (Available in December 1996.) #CCBCFPD

Nonmember: $11.95; ADA Member: $9.55

American Diabetes Association Complete Guide to Diabetes

Finally, all areas of diabetes self-care are covered in the pages of one book. Whether you have type I or type II diabetes, you'll learn all about symptoms and causes, diagnosis and treatment, handling emergencies, complications and prevention, achieving good blood sugar control, and more. You'll also discover advice on nutrition, exercise, sex, pregnancy, travel, family life, coping, and health insurance. 464 pages. Hardcover. Conveniently indexed for quick reference to any topic. #CSMCGD

Nonmember: $29.95; ADA Member: $23.95

How to Get Great Diabetes Care

This book explains the American Diabetes Association's Standards of Care and informs you—step-by-step—of the importance of seeking medical attention that meets these standards. You'll learn about special concerns and treatment options for diabetes-related diseases and conditions. #CSMHGGDC

Nonmember: $11.95; ADA Member: $9.55

Reflections on Diabetes

A collection of stories written by people who have learned from the experience of living with diabetes. Selected from the *Reflections* column of *Diabetes Forecast* magazine, these stories of success, struggle, and pain will inspire you. #CSMROD

Nonmember: $9.95; ADA Member: $7.95

Sweet Kids: How to Balance Diabetes Control and Good Nutrition with Family Peace

At last! A professionally developed collection of advice for parents and caregivers of children with diabetes. Learn all about nutrition and meal planning in diabetes: food, diabetes, and proper development; special areas of concern, such as low blood sugar; self-care techniques for caregivers of children with diabetes; much more. Take advantage of this practical way to educate yourself about how to properly care for a person with diabetes. #CSMSK
Nonmember: $14.95; ADA Member: $11.95

101 Tips for Staying Healthy with Diabetes (and Avoiding Complications)

Developing complications of diabetes is a constant threat without proper self-care. *101 Tips for Staying Healthy* offers the inside track on the latest tips, techniques, and strategies for preventing and treating complications. You'll find simple, practical suggestions for avoiding complications through close blood-sugar control, plus easy-to-follow treatment strategies for slowing and even halting the progression of existing complications. Helpful illustrations with each tip. #CSMFSH
Nonmember: $12.50; ADA Member: $9.95

Bestsellers

Diabetes A to Z

In clear, simple terms, you'll learn all about blood sugar, complications, diet, exercise, heart disease, insulin, kidney disease, meal planning, pregnancy, sex, weight loss, and much more. Alphabetized for quick reference. #CGFDAZ
Nonmember: $9.95; ADA Member: $7.95

Managing Diabetes on a Budget

For less than $10 you can begin saving hundreds and hundreds on your diabetes self-care. An inexpensive, sure-fire collection of "do-it-this-way" tips and hints to save you money on everything from medications and diet to exercise and health care. #CSMMDOAB
Nonmember: $7.95; ADA Member: $6.25

The Fitness Book: For People with Diabetes

You'll learn how to exercise to lose weight, exercise safely, increase your competitive edge, get your mind and body ready to exercise, much more. #CSMFB
Nonmember $18.95; ADA Member: $14.95

Raising a Child with Diabetes

Learn how to help your child adjust insulin to allow for foods kids like to eat, have a busy schedule and still feel healthy and strong, negotiate the twists and turns of being "different," accept the physical and emotional challenges life has to offer, and much more. #CSMRACWD

Nonmember: $14.95; ADA Member: $11.95

The Dinosaur Tamer

Enjoy 25 fictional stories that will entertain, enlighten, and ease your child's frustrations about having diabetes. Each tale warmly evaporates the fear of insulin shots, blood tests, going to diabetes camp, and more. Ages 8–12. #CSMDTAOS

Nonmember: $9.95; ADA Member: $7.95

101 Tips for Improving Your Blood Sugar

101 Tips offers a practical, easy-to-follow roadmap to tight blood sugar control. One question appears on each page, with the answers or "tips" below each question. Tips on diet, exercise, travel, weight loss, insulin injection, illness, sex and much more. #CSMTBBGC

Nonmember: $12.50; ADA Member $9.95

Order Toll-Free! 1–800–ADA–ORDER (232–6733)
VISA • MasterCard • American Express

Or send your check or money order to:
American Diabetes Association
ATTN: Order Fulfillment Department
P.O. Box 930850
Atlanta, GA 31193–0850

Shipping & Handling:
up to $30 . . . . add $3.00
$30.01–$50 . . . . add $4.00
above $50 . . . . add 8% of order

Allow 2–3 weeks for shipment. Add $3 to shipping & handling for each extra shipping address. Add $15 for each overseas shipment. Prices subject to change without notice.

Also available in bookstores nationwide

You'll Get Fabulous *New* Recipe Ideas and More . . . Each Month in Diabetes Forecast!

Successful diabetes control is in your hands! *Diabetes Forecast* features exciting, original recipes complete with exchange values.

And there's more! You'll read the latest research news, learn how to avoid complications . . . there's even a children's corner!

Plus, when you subscribe, you become a member of the American Diabetes Association. You'll receive a discount on books, access to the Information Hotline, membership in your local ADA affiliate, and more great benefits in addition to your monthly issue of *Diabetes Forecast*.

Now That's a Recipe for Success!

☐ Yes, I want to join the American Diabetes Association. I've enclosed $24 annual dues.* I will receive 12 issues of *Diabetes Forecast*, membership in my local affiliate, and discounts on all ADA publications.

Name _____

Address _____

City _____ State _____ Zip _____

Telephone _____

Please mail this form with payment to:
American Diabetes Association
General Membership
P.O. Box 363
Mt. Morris, IL 61054–0363

ABK097